# Building Website With

# JOOMLA! 2.5

## A Game Changer for Young Entrepreneurs

"You do not need to be
a programmer;
All you need is basic
Computer and internet
Knowledge to develop an
Impressive and high
Quality website in
Record time"

## AK SHEHU

PARTRIDGE
A Penguin Random House Company

Abdulwahab Yusuf Shehu (CEO A.Y. Identities Nigeria) - Editor
Isai Amuthan Krishnan - Proofreader
Janine Perez - Publishing Consultant
Shelly Edmunds - Publishing Services Associate
Carlo Angelo Tuvilla - Cover Designer
Jimmy Achapero Jr. - Interior Designer

- Joomla! is Free Software released under the GNU General Public License.
- The Joomla!® name and symbol are registered trademarks of Open Source Matters, Inc. in the United States and other countries.
- The Joomla! trademarks used herein are used under a limited license granted by Open Source Matters, the trademark holder.
- The author and publisher are in no way affiliated with Open Source Matters, Inc. or The Joomla Project.
- This book and it's content is not affiliated with, warranted by, reviewed by or otherwise endorsed by The Joomla! Project.

**To order additional copies of this book, contact**
Toll Free 800 101 2657 (Singapore)
Toll Free 1 800 81 7340 (Malaysia)
orders.singapore@partridgepublishing.com

www.partridgepublishing.com/singapore

# Contents

Dedication ........................................................................iv

Acknowledgement .............................................................v

Preface .............................................................................vi

A Game Changer for Young Entrepreneurs .....................viii

Introduction....................................................................xi

Chapter 1    Some Terms & Basic Structures of Joomla! .........1

Chapter 2    New Features in Joomla! 2.5 .........................13

Chapter 3    Installing Your Joomla! 2.5...........................27

Chapter 4    Understanding Categories in Joomla! 2.5 .........55

Chapter 5    Creating Your Articles & Menus ....................61

Chapter 6    Making your Site Dynamic with
             Component, Module & Plugins ......................83

Chapter 7    Using Templates & Extensions for Your
             Joomla! Site.............................................107

Chapter 8    Working with Users & Permissions in
             Joomla! 2.5............................................ 119

Chapter 9    Understanding Global Configuration,
             Check In & Statuses..................................129

Chapter 10   Exporting & Importing Joomla! 2.5
             Database from your PC to another PC.............137

Credits & Appendix...........................................................143

Appendix A: Key Resources ..............................................144

Appendix B: Some Organizations that Uses Joomla!............145

About the Author .............................................................146

# Dedication

*I would like to dedicate this book to my lovely Mother,
Hajiya Maryam Shehu for her prayers*

*And to my Wonderful wife, Noor Farhan Najah*

*without her love, support and patience, none of this would
be possible.*

# Acknowledgement

Praise is to God, the Creator of all that exist. Thanks to Him for the ability he gave me in writing this second book.

I want to thank Mr. Abdulwahab Yusuf Shehu for his valuable input to this new book and Mr. Isai Amuthan Krishnan for helping me proofread the content of the book. A special thanks to Mr. Abdul-Aziz Tanko, Dr. Ali Salman and Noor Farhan Najah BT Ramlee for their inspiration and continued support while I put together this new Book.

I would like to also pay tribute to the Joomla! Developers for their continued efforts in putting together this powerful Content Management System—that is Joomla! 2.5.

In addition, special thank you to my Friend Muhammed Irfan Ishak for introducing me into Joomla!

And finally to all my family and friends who always encourage and believed I could do it.

# Preface

Joomla! has become one of the most powerful and popular content management system in the world, it is actively supported and continuously developed by user community around the world. It is important to know that this great software is FREE and enriched with great tools for everyone who wants to create really cool, dynamic and interactive website of all kinds. Even novice can use Joomla! to create professional website, it can be challenging sometimes to get beyond the basics of Joomla! to create a site that meets your needs but this book provides a broad and thorough introduction to Web design using Joomla! 2.5. It is intended mainly for any person with basic knowledge of computer and internet who wish to develop personal website or other kind of websites. It presents a systematic account of the World Wide Web, which will serve as a foundation for anyone setting out on a career as a professional Website Developer.

Since my first book *"Building Website with Joomla 1.5 in 60 minutes"* was published in 2012, it has sold reasonably well, and received a very good response from its readers who applauded the simplicity and its clear instructions. Several readers especially young entrepreneurs and students were generous enough to say that the book has greatly impacted on their lives.

For this book which is focusing on the new Joomla! 2.5 version Showcase the new features which includes the styles, menu system, category system, User Management and access levels and many great features. There is a dedicated chapter that highlights the new features on the Joomla! 2.5.

This book is written for you to learn Joomla! 2.5 as fast as possible and I must thank you for deciding to read this book.

It is important that you read this book from A-Z, and all you have to do is simply read a page, do what it says and go ahead. You will be a confident Joomla! user after completing all the steps and tasks in this book.

Just as I said in my first book, when I first came across Joomla! I found it difficult to install and difficult to learn how it works generally. It was even more complicated to learn how to customize the website as per my requirement. In that period, there were many tutorials which explained different tasks, but not a single one explained how to install, administer or even modify Joomla! website to my needs. Hence, I learned Joomla! in a more complex way by trying out different tutorials, trying different buttons in the administrator Panel, and seeing what happens in the site. I gradually became proficient in making and administrating Joomla! websites. It took me months to go through all this processes.

I have written this book in such a way that you will learn how to use Joomla! within minutes. If you read this Book three times from *beginning to end* and do what it says, you will be able to make any type of Joomla! website.

# A Game Changer for Young Entrepreneurs

I n a statement by Barbara Kasumu from Elevations Network Speaking on youth employment, said:

> *"Vocational and technical training qualifications need to be valued at the same level as traditional academic routes. Education alone does not guarantee employment outcomes and more must be done to ensure that work experience is fully integrated into a young person's learning experience."* Source: *http://thecommonwealth.org*

I now come to realize that it is important for us to become self-reliant and engage in entrepreneurship. What is Entrepreneurship? *It is the capacity and willingness to develop, organize and manage a business venture along with any of its risks in order to make a profit*—According to Business Dictionary. We need to empower ourselves with skills and venture into business, I don't necessarily mean Big Business, No! Starting Small is good enough. Many of the big companies we see today started small like Microsoft, Apple Inc. to mention just few. Hence, putting our skills into practice will serve as a self-starter and a *"Game Changer"* for youths around the world. Many youths have graduated from universities, colleges with good grades but ended up without the suitable jobs, when you have skills, talent and great ideas you don't need to wait for any company to hire you. Believe me, Government alone cannot provide jobs for all; however, you can start by setting up a small scale business in your community.

By acquiring skills like Joomla! Today, you can confidently approach any Company, Restaurants and even Celebrities with a proposal to create website for them—of course you have to dress nice to give your potential clients a good impression ☺. Now that technology and internet is the most effective medium of doing business, many companies, be it small or large want an online presence and that's where you come in. Different companies are looking for the development of their corporate websites, which can be developed from Joomla! with much ease. With your Joomla! Skills; sky will not be your limit!

Having the skills and knowledge of web development will help you a long way because you will be able to start up your own Web Development Business as well as become a Joomla! Trainer. Being a Joomla! Trainer, you could help spread knowledge and empower youths not only in your community but around the world. As for me:

*"I take pride in sharing my skills and knowledge especially in Joomla! & Entrepreneurship; I have empowered youths, student, Teachers, Businessmen & Women, Friends & Colleagues on the effectiveness of Using of Joomla! Web Development in Africa— Nigeria to be precise and in Malaysia where I currently live"*

Conclusively, Joomla! Web development skills are indispensable for youths irrespective of their fields of study or academic background; Technical or NOT, because at the end you will realize that you need an online presence for your kind of profession. However, when it comes to Website Development &

Design, Joomla! Offers *"Endless Possibilities"* on the Web. Thus, I strongly recommend you to read this book from beginning to end and practice every step to get yourself equip with Latest Joomla! web development skills.

# Introduction

Internet has become one of the most flourishing industries in recent years, and everyone wants to get into it. Many companies have set up websites for people to visit and browse through their services or products and Countless companies have also posted the history of their company and their accomplishments on websites so that people can be aware of them. But if you were to engage into the internet market, will it not take much time to get everything organized and at the same time, build the website? Don't Worry! *Joomla!* is here to make it simple and easy for you to develop and design your own website. Hence, you don't have to pay to get it done by web Design Company . . . ☺

When you first think about having a website for yourself or for your business, it might be a bit confusing how to go about it. You don't have to worry about giving a company to develop a website for you; *Joomla!* makes life easy for you. This section will guide you through some easy key points to start building your Joomla! website. I have structured these points as follows:

✓ *Why do you need a website?*

✓ *How do I get started with Joomla! 2.5?*

- ✓ *What do you know about Joomla!?*

- ✓ *What is Content Management System (CMS)*

- ✓ *What Joomla! 2.5 can do*

- ✓ *Who Uses Joomla!?*

- ✓ *How do I install Joomla!?*

- ✓ *How should I set up my site?*

- ✓ *Picking a Template*

- ✓ *Organizing Content*

- ✓ *Creating Navigation and many more.*

## Why Do You Need A Website?

You definitely should ask yourself, do I need a website? Yes, you might think! But why? If you don't have a clear goal for having or developing a website, your website will not be organized and will have no value. You must identify your goals or else you will be building site with no bearing. But what shall I use exactly for my website?

To tell you the truth, Joomla! is an excellent solution for your website development and design. It has thousands of *FREE extensions* that will suit your need in the development and design of your website. I strongly recommend you to go for it.

## How Do I Get Started With Joomla! 2.5?

Joomla! is free anyone can use, share, and support. To download the latest Joomla! 2.5 version go to *http://www.joomla.org/download.html*. I will recommend you to download the full package.

## What Do You Know About Joomla!?

The word Joomla is derived from the word *Jumla* from the African language of Swahili which means "*all together*". Joomla! is a development of the successful system Mambo and it is used all over the world for simple homepages and for complex corporate websites as well. It is easy to install, easy to manage and very reliable. The Joomla! team has organised and reorganised itself throughout the last seven years.

- ✓ From 2005 to 2009, Joomla 1.0 was developed up to version 1.0.15 and that development was officially laid off in September 2009.

- ✓ From 2005 until 2012, Joomla 1.5, was introduced as a stable version in January 2008, and officially 'end of life' in April but was extended to September 2012 because users of Joomla! 1.5 asked for an extension.

- ✓ From 2008 until 2011, Joomla 1.6 was developed. A stable version has been available since January 2011.

- ✓ In July 2011 Joomla 1.7 was released

- ✓ Joomla 2.5 is the first long term release since Joomla 1.5 was released. The next stable version will be the Joomla! 3.5.

*"Joomla!, together with Drupal and WordPress, are the most used open source web content management system in the world"*

Joomla! is an award-winning content management system (CMS), which enables you to build Web sites and powerful online applications. Many aspects, including its ease-of-use and extensibility, have made Joomla! the most popular Web site software available. Best of all, Joomla! is an open source solution that is freely available to everyone.

Joomla! is an *"open source* "Content Management System. An open Source means that anyone can contribute to the code, improve it, or distribute it. This means the platform is a living project being created and improved by a community of developers all over the world.

A content management system uses a database to place content into designated places on the web page. It's dynamic and in real time. Joomla! is easy but powerful.

The software itself is absolutely FREE, but there are some extensions that you might need to buy to really meet your website requirement. However, many extensions are FREE. Read the extension chapter to understand better.

## What is Content Management System (CMS)?

A content management system (CMS) is software that keeps track of every piece of content on your Website; much like your local public library keeps track of books and stores them. Content can be simple text, photos, music, video, documents, or just about anything you can think of. A major advantage of using a CMS is that it requires almost no technical skill or knowledge to manage.

## What Joomla! 2.5 Can Do

Joomla! is used all over the world to power about 23.5 million Websites of all shapes and sizes. Joomla! can do the following:

- ✓ E-commerce and online reservations

- ✓ Government applications

- ✓ Small business Web sites

- ✓ Non-profit and organizational Websites

- ✓ Non-profit and organizational Websites

- ✓ Community-based portals

- ✓ School and church Web sites

- ✓ Corporate Web sites or portals

- ✓ Online magazines, newspapers, and publications, and many more.

## Who Uses Joomla!?

The following are just few from millions of organization who use Joomla!

- ➤ UNISEL University Selangor—http://www.unisel.edu.my/

- ➤ Guaranty Trust Bank Uses Joomla—http://gtbank.com/

- ➤ Malaysia Immigration—http://www.imi.gov.my

- ➤ Monaco yacht show—http://www.monacoyachtshow.com

- ➤ Barnes & noble—https://nookdeveloper.barnesandnoble.com

- ➤ U.K ministry of defense—http://www.stabilisationunit.gov.uk

- ➤ High Court Of Australia Uses Joomla—www.hcourt.gov.au

- ➤ Eiffel Tower Uses Joomla—http://www.tour-eiffel.fr/

*And many more at http://joomlagov.info/*

Joomla! is designed to be an easy-to-install software and you can set it up even if you're not an advanced user. Many Web hosting services offer a real time *single-click installation*, getting your new site up and running in just a few minutes. Live!

Since Joomla! is so easy to use, as a Web designer or developer, you can quickly build sites for your clients. Then, with a minimal amount of instruction, you can empower your clients to easily manage their own sites themselves.

*"After mastering Joomla! you might want to develop website for some clients. However, your clients might need specialized functionality, Joomla! is highly extensible and thousands of extensions (most for free under the <u>GPL license</u>) are available in the <u>Joomla Extensions Directory</u>. To see more on this go to <u>http://extensions.joomla.org/</u>"*

## How Do I Set Up My Joomla! 2.5 Website?

Many people find it difficult to set up their site because it is one of the hardest parts of Joomla! There are many options and can be overpowering. Joomla! has three important elements which are:

1. *Template*—This gives the site a great look and with all the design that is visible to visitors.

2. *Content*—This is the main area where information's are displayed.

3. *Modules*—They contains the menus and can be set to any position within the template.

The next picture shows what the three elements represent in Joomla!

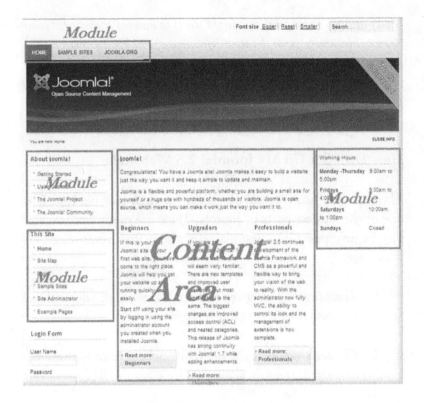

## How Do I Pick A Template in Joomla!?

To pick a template for your Joomla! Site, you will have to choose from any one of the available templates in Joomla! or install a new one; there are thousands of free Joomla! for you to download.

However, Joomla! 2.5 come with free templates for front-end and back-end. To get started, just use one of these, then you can later install a 3$^{rd}$ party template of which there are thousands available. You may choose to buy professional ones or use the free one's which you can get online.

*Note:* *There are good free Joomla! Template on the internet, I would recommend you go through the free ones before considering buying a commercial template. Always check the version of the template before using it (this book talks about Joomla! 2.5 version).*

## The Content

The main content of the site is made up of article and articles are Webpages that displays information like text, images and so on. Content or articles need some containers and these are called in Joomla! 2.5 "Categories". Though not all websites require categories for their contents, it depends on the kind of site you intend to create. However, these categories can have many articles. However, you can have as many categories as you want on your website.

## Creating Navigation

*"You will not be making any sense if your site doesn't have navigation. Visitors who will visit your site need to click through links, so it is indispensible to have links on your site. This can be the menu links otherwise nothing will be seen in your site."*

Joomla! has thousands of 3rd party extensions, ranging from online reservation, Project Management, Student Management System, Appointment system, Tracking System, e-commerce, Forums and many more. Some are free and some are commercial.

This introductory part only highlights some of the important points that you need to know in other to learn Joomla!2.5. Take your time to Read this book to get more insight about developing website with Joomla! 2.5. And as you read and practice what the book says, Pay more attention to how to create new Articles (webpages), Modules, Menus, Changing Templates and Installing Extension. If you follow the steps, then you are "Good 2 Go"☺!

**CHAPTER 1**

# Some Terms & Basic Structures of Joomla!

T his chapter will highlight some important structure of Joomla! 2.5 so that you can become familiar with them as you move on with your Joomla! practice. It will also allow you to know some key terms even before the installation of Joomla!

## Back-End (Administrator Panel)

The Administrator Back-end (Control Panel) is the first page that display when an administrator, (could be a *Manager, Administrator, or Super Administrator*) logs into the Back-end of the Joomla! Website.

This is your administration area; therefore, I call it your Workshop. You can give registered users the right to work in your back-end. This privilege is mostly limited to several employees in an organisation, who administers some the website task like updating contents and so on.

To login to the administrator panel; type 'localhost/yoursitename/administrator' in the browser, for example: localhost/myfirstsite/administrator.

The actual content of the **Control Panel** that each level of administrator sees depends upon their Access Level. A Manager sees less than an Administrator, who in turn sees less than the Super Administrator (who sees it all and has complete control over it!). This difference extends to the actual functions that each can carry out.

After you logged in successfully, you'll have access to the administrator panel, which is structured according to your user rights. The next image shows the ***Administrator control panel (workshop).***

At any time when the Menu bar is available at the top of the page (i.e, you are not editing or taking any action in a page), you can return to the *Control Panel* by clicking the *Home* button in the top menu bar.

3

## Front-End (Site View)

The front-end means the areas of the website as visitors or registered users of the website see it, which is the actual website view. A registered user normally works only in the front-end. Basically like how goods are being displayed in the shops for customers to see. See image below.

## Database (DB)

Joomla! also needs a database. During the installation procedure, the Joomla! web installer creates 61 tables in your specified database. All content of the website will be managed in these tables. Have a look at the next image to understand better.

Content here refers to the text and the configuration setting however, the table's shown in the above image are displayed by *phpMyAdmin*. This is part of WAMP and its available when you click on the *localhost* on your task bar, you will be prompted with a list of items and there you can see the *phpMyAdmin*. Alternatively, you may type '*localhost/phpmyadmin* on the browser to view the page. Additionally you can use this software to back-up your database by simply creating a SQL Dump, meaning you can export your database also to your local PC.

## Files

Joomla! consists of hundreds of files, Images, CSS files, JavaScript files PHP scripts, and a many more. You probably would have noticed when you unpacked (unzip) the compressed package of Joomla! and copied it into the folder. Essentially, you have installed two Joomla! packages: for the front-end and for the back-end. The 'Back-end' is located in the *administrator* folder.

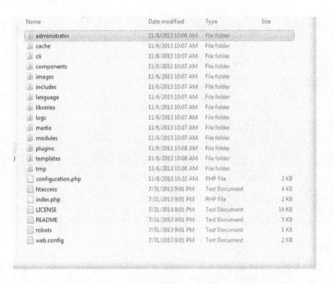

| Name | Date modified | Type | Size |
|------|---------------|------|------|
| administrator | 11/6/2013 10:06 AM | File folder | |
| cache | 11/6/2013 10:07 AM | File folder | |
| cli | 11/6/2013 10:07 AM | File folder | |
| components | 11/6/2013 10:07 AM | File folder | |
| images | 11/6/2013 10:07 AM | File folder | |
| includes | 11/6/2013 10:07 AM | File folder | |
| language | 11/6/2013 10:07 AM | File folder | |
| libraries | 11/6/2013 10:07 AM | File folder | |
| logs | 11/6/2013 10:07 AM | File folder | |
| media | 11/6/2013 10:07 AM | File folder | |
| modules | 11/6/2013 10:07 AM | File folder | |
| plugins | 11/6/2013 10:08 AM | File folder | |
| templates | 11/6/2013 10:08 AM | File folder | |
| tmp | 11/6/2013 10:08 AM | File folder | |
| configuration.php | 11/6/2013 10:32 AM | PHP File | 2 KB |
| htaccess | 7/31/2013 9:01 PM | Text Document | 4 KB |
| index.php | 7/31/2013 9:01 PM | PHP File | 2 KB |
| LICENSE | 7/31/2013 9:01 PM | Text Document | 18 KB |
| README | 7/31/2013 9:01 PM | Text Document | 5 KB |
| robots | 7/31/2013 9:01 PM | Text Document | 1 KB |
| web.config | 7/31/2013 9:01 PM | Text Document | 2 KB |

This folder is addressed when you call /administrator in the browser. Inside that folder are other folders like *language, cache, modules components and templates.* The specific back-end files are stored in these directories. You will find the same folder names again outside the *administrator* folder. These folders contain the front-end files (site). It is a clear separation between *back-end* and *front-end* files, note that these are not really two Joomla! packages. But for instance, all files that is uploaded with the *Media Manager* will be saved in the */media* folder. Make sure all files are well backed-up.

## Elements of Joomla!

The structure of Joomla! is very sophisticated yet simple and efficient. The assumption Joomla! has is that you want to write an article and such article usually contains a title, text and some configuration settings. Read on to understand these great elements.

## *The Article*

One of the most important parts of a website is the content. However in Joomla! an Article is a piece of content consisting of text (HTML), possibly with links to other resources. For example, images, links etc can be within an article. Articles can be displayed in single or list view. On the front-page of your installed Joomla! website you will see any of your created articles. These articles are maintained using the article manager in the back-end of the Joomla! *Administrator panel*. In Joomla!, article are referred to as the content in which you want to display in the site. See the next image to understand how the articles looks like when displayed in the front-page.

Articles can be arranged in a certain way. The top article is displayed by using the full width of the website. The remaining articles are placed below in three columns. If the articles are too long, you may insert a *read more* link. This representation is a list view. By clicking on the *read more* link you will be redirected to the single representation of that article where you can read the full article in a single page. The type of display can be changed by setting *options* in the back-end, note that only user with access rights can execute this settings.

> **Note:** *Articles can be published (publish) or not published (unpublish). You can feature articles on your Front-page, you can archive them or put them in the trash and retrieve them at later time. You can also copy and move them too, all is possible with Joomla!*

## *The Categories*

For you to have your articles displayed noticeably, you must create categories, and then assign an article to them. Each of the articles can be assigned to just one category. Articles from one or multiple categories can be assigned to one menu item and displayed in many ways. Once you click on the menu item or any other menu, all articles from different categories will be shown. Mostly such is used by online newspapers or restaurants for instance, when you click on *Vegetarian* you will get all categorized articles for this topic. Take a look at the category trees:

✓  Asia—(Category)

- Sports Asia → (Article)
- Talk Asia → (Article)

✓  Africa—(Category)

- African Sports → (Article)
- Voice of Africa → (Article)

## Understanding Components

Component is one of the extension in Joomla!. Components are the main functional units of Joomla! They can be seen as mini-applications. The components are Joomla!'s content elements or applications that are usually displayed in the center of the main content area of a template. However, this depends on the design of the template you are using. Components are core elements of Joomla!'s functionality. Some of these core elements include Banners, Contact Component and Smart Search. There are thousands of components that you can download to enhance your Joomla! website.

## Understanding Module

Modules are the blocks of contents in your site and are distinctively separate from your main content area. For example, a module may appear to the left, right, top, or down or below your main article content. The Module Manager allows you to customize each module to your "Preference". You can create as many modules with smart functions as you need and position them on the predefined area in the template. Each module in Joomla! has some constant features. Modules have more individual parameters but these are the most important ones to understand first. Some of the fields you will see in **every module:** *Title Show Title, Status, Position, Module Class Suffix, Start &Finish Publishing, Menu Assignment and Ordering.*

## Understanding User

Users are important part of your website development and are needed to create content. At least one user is registered on each

Joomla! site, which is the one you created during the installation, with the rights to configure everything on your site (*Super Administrator*). Depending on the user's rights, he can work in front-end or back-end or both to write an article. Each user requires a *username*, an *email* address and a *password*. Every user can be assigned to any user group as well as to any access level. This enables the user to create articles that are only visible to certain user groups.

## Understanding Navigation

To understand the website, you will need navigation with corresponding links. In Joomla! This is called *menu*. You may create as many menus as you want and nest them into as many different ways as you wish. Based on the template you use, each menu is a module which can be positioned on a provided area in the template.

## The Plug-ins

A plug-in provides practical services but is usually invisible to the visitors of the site. A **WYSIWYG** editor, for example, is a plug-in. Plug-ins are extensions, which can be installed unlimited amount of times. The core package already consists of numerous useful plug-ins.

## Understanding Templates

A template is the graphical pattern for your website. It mostly consists of HTML and CSS files. Joomla! provides several templates for you to choose from. Templates are configurable, which allows you to upload a different logo, change the background colour and other setting to enrich your website looks. Each template provides areas where modules can be positioned. The next image shows a template.

## *Options*

You will need individual configuration settings for your website; this is called *options*. These are applied to the whole website, for *users, categories, modules and components*. You will always find an icon named *Options* at the top right of the page.

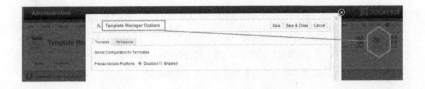

It also provides you with the possibility to see the position of modules (*Figure 8*) by inserting *http://localhost/index.php?tp=1*. The *tp* stands for template position.

# CHAPTER 2

# New Features in Joomla! 2.5

Joomla! 2.5 was released in January 2011 and it is the successor of Joomla! 1.5. It is expected to be a long term release until around winter 2014. The 1.6 and 1.7 versions of Joomla! were short term releases and they paved the way to Joomla 2.5. However, there are many new significant features in 2.5 including new search functionality, multi-database support and update notification. Many people in the Joomla! Community has contributed to making these new features possible. This chapter discusses the new features in Joomla! 2.5.

## Brand New Administrator Interface

New administrator interface is redesigned to allow you work conveniently.

## It Supports Other Databases

Joomla! has traditionally run on the MySQL database. If your company has a different type of SQL database, such as MS SQL, then you'd have to make changes to the Joomla! software to make it work. This process makes it difficult, but Joomla! has been rewritten so that different drivers can be written for different versions of SQL databases. Current drivers exist for the MySQL and MS SQL databases, with PostgreSQL, Oracle, SQLite and PDO drivers close to being ready.

## Joomla! Update Notification

Because of the various requests from the community to enable Joomla! notify site administrator when Joomla! needs to be updated. Now in Joomla! 2.5 Site administrators will be able to see as soon as they login if Joomla! is out of date. They can then click the button and be taken to the one-click update to Joomla!. A second (2) icon does the same thing for any non-core components that are set up for the one-click updating by their developers.

## Ability to Choose if Administrator Gets Email When New Users Register

It is now possible to choose whether the administrator gets a new message when a user creates an account.

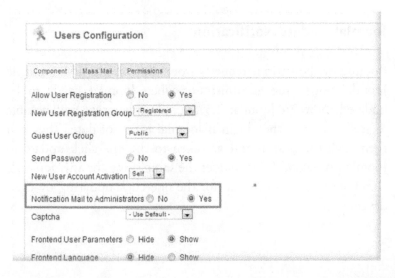

## Better Choices for your Website offline Mode

A Joomla! Logo has always been the display when you put a site offline. This leads to confusion on whose site it is. In order to fix it, you had to provide a custom file in your template. Now With this new feature, no image is displayed by default and you can upload/select any image of your choice to be displayed wen your website is offline.

## Better Performance in Menu Item Edit Page

The extensive options in *"Select a Menu Item Type"* are not loaded unless you need them.

## Enhanced Status Display in Back-end

The footprint of the status displays has been reduced to prevent overcrowding (in English).

## User Notes

Now you can attach notes to users as well as assign dates to the users. These manual dates can be used for whatever you want, whether it's a date for reviewing the user, the last date you reviewed a user or for something entirely different. You can change the label for the date using the Language Overrides. You can have multiple notes per user and the notes can be in different categories.

## Better Flexibility Filtering by Category in the Article Manager

In previous versions of Joomla!, you could filter by category when looking at articles. However, you didn't have a way of selecting a category and getting all the articles that are in that category and its subcategories. In Joomla! 2.5, selecting a category in the articles manager will include its subcategories down to the depth you select. If you only want the single category, you can select a level of 1.

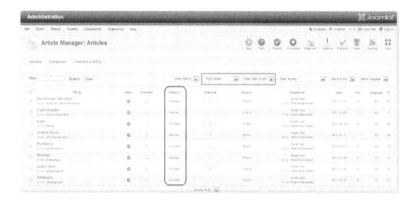

## The New Search Function

Joomla! 2.5 has added an exciting new natural language search function, this is based on Finder, which was developed by jXtended. This feature incorporated auto-completion and stemming. Stemming is the ability for the search to use the root of the word you entered to locate matches. While there is still work to be done, this search is also much better at searching in languages other than English. This new search is faster and more versatile than the standard search. The data is indexed to get this flexibility and speed. New plugins are required to use this search. By default, the standard search is active and this new search is disabled. You can enable the plugin and index your files when the extensions you want to search have the new plugins.

## User Registrations With CAPTCHA

A CAPTCHA plugin using the *reCAPTCHA* service can be enabled. Once you sign up for free with *reCAPTCHA* and enter your keys, you can enable CAPTCHA on new user registrations. It could also be used by other extensions needing CAPTCHA.

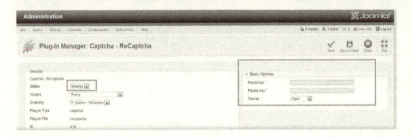

## Easier Handling For Simple Layouts

You can now attach an image for the intro text to use in blog and featured layouts, an image for the full article text and up to three links for the full article layout. This means that your content creators won't have to fuss with an image in the text and your article format will be cleaner and more consistent.

## Multilanguage

You can override the default language strings in a new manager in the backend.

## Mobile

The Beez core template comes with mobile enhancements. However 2.5 now allow templates to be compatible with mobile display.

## Smart Search

Search is "reinvented" in Joomla! 2.5 with Finder. The new finder component works with a search index.

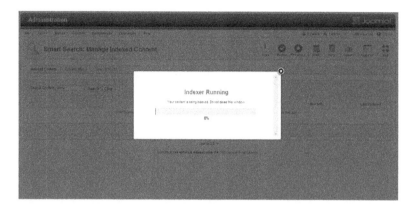

The Finder pre-searches your content. Search results are scored dynamically based on the context and frequency of search terms. The most relevant content will always be listed at the top of the results. It suggests alternative phrases and its pluggable adapter system allows installing new search adapters which provide support for standard Joomla! content and many other types of documents. ***Custom search filters*** allows you to provide contextual searching when your visitor is looking at particular sections of your Web site.

## The New 2.5 Features compared to Joomla! 1.5

When you compare ***Joomla! 1.5 with 2.5,*** the differences is clear and there is a long list of new *features* and enhancements.

It's important to also have a look at the most important change in Joomla 1.6 and 1.7

✓ There will no longer be any sections. **Categories can be nested** as deeply as you would like.

✓ The **access concept** is totally rebuilt.

The existing user groups used in *Joomla! 1.5* are still the same in Joomla! 2.5 but they can be enhanced and renamed. Unlimited access levels can also be defined there. User groups can be assigned to access levels and different groups can then be assigned to various access levels.

## Multiprocessing

Copy and move operations and the allocation of access levels can now be done in a batch process.

## Updates per Mouse Click

A simple feature. The system detects available updates and initiates them by clicking on the corresponding button.

## Templates

There have been many changes in the area of templates. There are now two administrator templates and three website templates.

## Template Styles

Sometimes you may want to display a template with different options. You may want to create a page with a red background and another page with a blue one. Therefore, you will need template styles. Create as many versions (styles) of a template with different settings as you like and assign them to a menu link.

## Template Layouts

Sometimes you may want to display only the output of a component or a module in a different layout without hacking the template. That's possible with template layouts.

## Consistent User Interface

A very good example is the general save dialogue.

- **Save:** *content will be saved, you remain in editing mode.*

- **Save & Close:** *content will be saved, you leave the editing mode.*

- **Save & New:** *content will be saved; a new, empty editing mask appears.*

- **Save as copy:** *content will be saved as a copy, you remain in the editing mask.*

## Minimum Requirements

The minimum requirements regarding your server environment and concerning your visitors' web browsers have increased.

Browser: Internet Explorer, version 7 or higher, Firefox, version 3 or higher, Safari, version 4 or higher

Server: PHP: minimum version PHP 5.2.4, MySQL: minimum version 5.04

## Legacy Mode

The legacy mode from Joomla! 1.5 is no longer necessary. Legacy mode allowed the execution of components originally developed for Joomla 1.0, which have only been adapted to Joomla! 1.5. The procedure of adapting old components is offset by the development of *native* Joomla! 1.5 and 2.5 components, which use the Joomla! *Framework.*

## Search Engine Optimization (SEO)

- You can now use unicode in URLs, which means you may now use special characters like 'ö' and 'ä' or Arabic or Hebrew characters in the URL.

- You can also allocate *meta text* and *keywords* to categories.

- A title of a site will be displayed following the name of the website in the browser.

## Modules

This can be published time-controlled. The assignment options to menu items have been extended.

## Multilingualism

Joomla! core now offers the possibility to create articles, categories and modules in several languages. With the new language switcher plug-in module you can filter the entire site for the selected language.

## New editor

Code Mirror is the new editor, which is supplied in addition to TinyMCE. It is not a WYSIWYG editor but offers a convenient way to work with *'code-like'* content, which will be displayed in colour and a structured way.

## Components

- The new redirect component enables redirections to URLs in order to avoid '404 not found' errors.

- The new search component provides an overview of the searched keywords and display results.

- The survey component has been eliminated.

## Who's online filters

Joomla! administrators can now show only the online users from a specific group if they want to. This can come really be convenient if you want to display the available administrators online for example.

There are many more very nice features like the possibility to place a background image into a module or to display articles with page breaks in a tab or slider layout.

*You will be convinced by now that Joomla! 2.5 is indeed great and powerful.*

# CHAPTER 3

# Installing Your Joomla! 2.5

## Installing a Web Server—WAMP

Joomla! 2.5 is the latest version and it is a web application that was written using PHP (PHP is a programming language used for web application, it's an open source) and hence it needs a "web server" to run. To make a Joomla! Site available on the World Wide Web, you need to host it on a web host. However, because you want to learn how to develop website using Joomla! 2.5, your own computer can be converted into a web server, after which you can then Install Joomla! 2.5 on it. Hence, you will need one basic thing to Install Joomla! 2.5 on your computer; you will be shown how to do this in this chapter.

To proceed with the installation of Joomla! 2.5 you need a WAMP Server for a Windows Operating System. WAMP (Windows Apache MySQL PHP) is a platform of Web development under Windows. Initially, installing a web server used to be problematic, especially because you had to manually configure it to run PHP. But not anymore, much thanks to WAMP—this is FREE software that installs Apache Web Server, PHP and MySQL on your computer and configures these three to work together. All you have to do is download it and install!

There are different versions available for different Operating System however, I would recommend you to download a copy of WAMP from this link http://en.kioskea.net/download/download-1318-wamp-server

Now you should run and install the web server as it's very simple to install, just follow the instruction as most of the process is just to "click" next until the finish.

> **Tip:** *To start WAMP server on your local PC, you have to double click on the server application either on your desktop or any location you have saved it. It's advisable to have a shortcut icon on your desktop for easy access. Anytime you intend to continue with your Joomla! 2.5 Site development, you must put on the Server First.*

## Installing Joomla! 2.5

After successfully following the instructions on installing the server above, now let's install Joomla! 2.5 to our Local PC. You can download the full package of Joomla 2.5 from this link http://www.joomla.org/download.html. After downloading, unzip the folder and rename the unzipped folder to your website name, for example "myfirstsite". The site name should not contain any space.

Now Copy the folder and paste "myfirstsite" folder to **www** directory in **WAMP**. See the screenshot

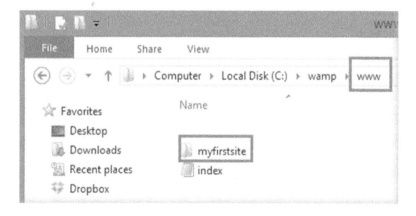

You can now access this folder from your web browser by typing 'localhost/myfirstsite'—without the Quote. You will be directed to the installation screen.

> ***Tip:*** *You can also "click" on the WAMP serve icon on your task bar and then click on 'localhost' after that you be directed to the WAMP server configuration page on your browser, there you can see your project (in this case it considered as your website). Remember after unzipping the Joomla 2.5 you downloaded, you changed the name to 'myfirstsite'? Yes, that is your website.*

You are almost there and it's absolutely simple from here, Joomla! 2.5 installations is made up of 7 Steps and these are:

***Step 1.*** The first thing you see in the browser is the installer which comes together with the language selection. Select your preferred language on the screen, and then click the **Next** button in the upper right corner of the page. See image below.

***Step 2.*** This is a series of system and server checks to ensure that Joomla! 2.5 will be able to install to your computer and function properly. The **top** section of items should all be **GREEN** and **'YES'**. Action will be needed in case any of the items not in green (they'll be "RED" and say "NO") to correct them. The section

at bottom of the items are not required, but is recommended to ensure that Joomla can operate efficiently. See image below.

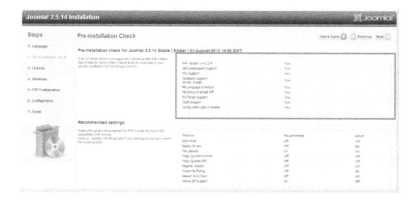

**Step 3.** Most if not all software product are licensed. Hence, Joomla! is licensed according to the GNU General Public License, version. This is the software license agreement for Joomla! use and simply requires you to click **Next** in the top right corner after reviewing. See image below.

**Step 4.** This is configuring the database connection for your Joomla! site. (Joomla 2.5.x now offers a random default prefix) This is helpful for security purposes. In this step, your database parameters will be requested. You can create any amount of databases in your local server environment. You have a

MySQL user with the name **root**. The user root is the MySQL administrator and can, therefore, do everything in your MySQL system. The password depends on your server environment (*no password is needed with WAMP*). You may **Use the following settings:**

✓ Database Type : mysqli

✓ Host name : localhost

✓ Username : root

✓ Password : Leave it blank if you are using your local PC

✓ Database Name : mfsbase (I only use "mfsbase" as an example, set your own database name)

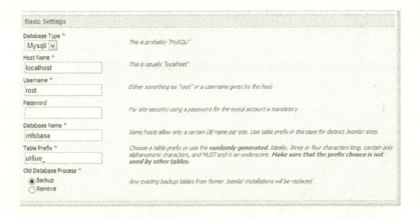

**Caution:** *Make sure you remember the database name you have created here; you will need it after you finish your website and ready to upload to a host server. You can only use the database name for only one project, make a different database name for different project.*

***Step 5***. This step is unnecessary for most sites and its need is usually identified if you find you cannot upload media or images or install Extensions. At a later time you can then add details directly within the **Global Configuration** in the Joomla! Administration pages. This step is **not** required on servers installed on a *Windows Operating System*. So, click **Next** to continue without doing anything on this step. See the next image.

***Step 6***. This is the **Site Main Configuration**. Here you **must** add the *Site Name, Admin Username, Admin Password, and Admin e-mail address*. If you are a novice (New) to Joomla! You should click on **Install the Sample Data**; this will help you with learning about Joomla! because your website will initially have some sample contents, in which you can delete or even edit at a later time when you are restructuring your website. However, this book aims at teaching you how to install and develop your Joomla! 2.5 by adding contents, modules, components, plugins and templates to enable you understand the concept of developing a website using this great software. See the next image for the **6ᵗʰ Step.**

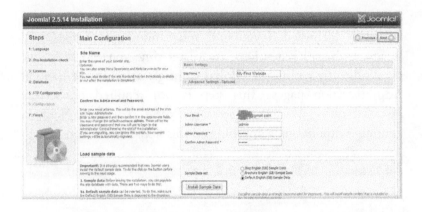

**Step 7.** This is the final step in the installation of Joomla! 2.5. Joomla! 2.5 is now installed! You **must** now remove the installation directory. This needs to be removed for security reasons to prevent anyone else from coming along and reinstalling Joomla over your existing site. Click the **Remove Installation Directory** button. This has become easier unlike in the Joomla! 1.5 versions which you have to go to the directory in the *C: Drive* to delete the installation folder. See the image below.

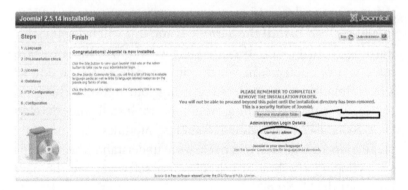

*Congratulations!* You have now successfully installed Joomla! 2.5 on your computer. Now that you have fully installed Joomla! 2.5 on your computer, you can now start configuring your new website and content.

To login to the Admin panel, remember your Username is: *admin* and your *Password* is known to you only. This is the password you set in the **6ᵗʰ step.**

In an event where you forgot to delete the installation directory, you will receive a reminder to do so instantly and then refresh the page.

> **Note:** *If you do not want to install the* **'Sample Data'**, *just click next to continue from the 6ᵗʰ Step to the final step. This means that at the end of the installation process, you will have a blank website and you need to build it from scratch. After the installation folder is deleted, you can either click on* **'Site'** *to view your new website or* **'Admin'** *to redirect to the Back-end of the website where you continue your site restructure.*

## How to Install Joomla! 2.5 Without the Sample Data?

Follow the same Steps above to install a fresh Joomla! 2.5 without Sample Data: in the *6ᵗʰ Step*, after adding the *Site Name, Admin Username, Admin Password, and Admin e-mail address*. Click **Nex**t and **DO NOT** click on the 'Install Sample Data'. This will allow you install Joomla! 2.5 Without any content in it and so you can start adding content, modules and other extensions you wish to suit your taste.

## An impressive View of the (Site) Front-End

You can now access the website by typing the address "localhost/myfirstsite" in your web browser. The view is the default Joomla! 2.5 site with the sample content. As you read and follow the steps in this book, you will see how to modify this new site according to your needs in the upcoming chapters. But for now, just feel free and navigate the site, clicking on different buttons and links trying them out. Have a look around, browse through a few options and try to acquaint yourself with your new site. Many features of Joomla! are being used on this website filled with *Sample Data*. The next image shows the view of the website after installation with the '*Sample Data*'.

## The Basics of Joomla!

Joomla! is Content Management System (CMS) software, which is used to manage contents of any type. However, to have a fully functional Joomla! 2.5 website you must have a database.

- All content, images are stored in the database.

- Whenever a guest visits the website, the front-end displays the contents stored in the database upon request from the guest r user.

- The administrative back-end of Joomla! allows you to edit the content of the website or create new content to it; you also can change the overall looks of the website from the admin-back end. This is however the ***workshop*** of your site.

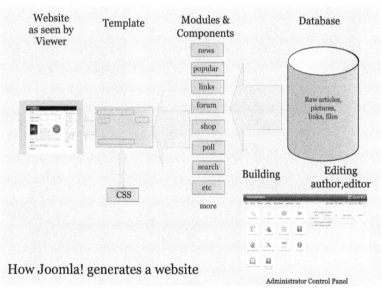

How Joomla! generates a website

*Source of image: Lloyd (2006) "Learn Joomla!"*

When you see the Joomla! site, its front-end displays some of the content stored in the database as seen in image above. All the data used in the whole website development are stored in the database. However, the administrative interface lets you edit the database; hence you have the absolute control over the entire site.

## Creating Your First Joomla! Website

Now that you have your Joomla! 2.5 installed in your computer and you have made yourself familiar with the contents and navigation from the Back-end (administrator Panel), it's time to create your new website

> **Note:** *The Back-end interface is different from the Joomla! 1.5, though most of the actions and steps are the same.*

Choose any name for your website, as for this book I am using my "My First Website". Writing your website name can be done in the Global Configuration. However, this website will only have **five** pages. We shall engage in a *4 Phase* action, these are:

✓ Writing the name of your website

✓ Creating content pages (Articles)

✓ Linking the created pages to Menus

✓ Removing unwanted content from the website.

*Tip: If you have installed the Joomla! 2.5 as described earlier in this chapter, then you can access your website by simply typing 'localhost/myfirstsite' in the browser—this will only show you the front-end of the site. For accessing the administrator interface (Back-end) of the website where you do all your restructuring, you have to type 'locahost/myfirstsite/administrator' on your web browser.*

## *Phase ONE:* Writing Your Site Name

Login with your username as *admin* and *password* as you set during the installation process of Joomla! the admin panel will be displayed as shown below:

- Click on the *'Global Configuration'* button.

- You will be shown different fields which will let you specify the name of your website.

- At this point use the "site name" field to write your website name. We have stated above to use "**My First Website**" as the name of the site.

- Clicks save after writing your site name. You should get a message saying **"configuration successfully saved"**

## *Phase TWO:* Creating the Content Pages

It is important to note that we are creating a simple content based website with just 5 pages. They are as follows:

1. About Us

2. What is Joomla!?

3. Using Joomla! 2.5

4. Why Joomla! 2.5?

5. Joomla! project

It has become even easier to create pages with Joomla! 2.5. To start creating content pages in Joomla! 2.5 **Go** to the administrative interface **"click"** on the **"Add New Article"** Button. You can also do this by going to → **Content** → **Article Manager** → **Add New Article"**. We shall discuss more about Article in a later chapters. If you are familiar with Joomla! 1.5, you will notice changes in the interface as well as the positions where the items are located. As I have mentioned earlier, most of the action is same with the Joomla 1.5 but the interface is different with some additional features. See the image below.

The result after clicking the **Add New Article** is an interface where you now have to type all the text and add images that you wish to display on the page. The Article interface looks as shown in the next image:

After typing the title and text, in the upper pane, below the title, select "**Uncategorized**" as a category. This category was by default created during installation of the *Sample Data*. The field "**Featured**" shows whether the content should be displayed in the featured blog layout (that is, in the website view) which is mostly used as the front page. By default is set to **No**, thus leave it as **No**. In the editor window, you may now enter your text after you finish click **Save & Close**. The TinyMCE editor comes with Joomla! Once you install Joomla!

After saving the page, you will be redirected to the "**Article Manager**" where you can still edit the existing article, delete or make any new article.

To create a new Content page or **Article,** click on the **New** button on the top right in the "**Article Manager**", See the image below.

*Tip: Now that you have successfully created the first Article (content page) repeat the step above to keep creating the pages. Do this process for the other four Pages.*

One impressive feature about Joomla! Is that, it lets you write article or pages using the reach text editor as shown in the next image.

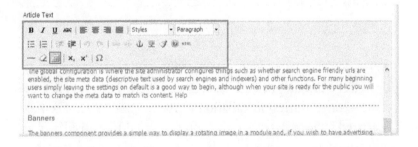

This gives you the total control of how you want the looks of your pages/articles to be, just the way you like it!. The text editor is something like the Microsoft Word processing software. You can insert images, links, emoticons, and many more features.

However, if you intend to add an **image** to your article or content, you will need to upload it from your Computer. To do this Go to the **Article Manager** or (**Content → Article Manager**). Select the article's title and the edit form will open. Below the editor window you will find the Image button. This button launches a dialog box to upload an image. You can choose between existing images or upload new ones, but primarily, you have to put the cursor to the point where you want the image to be placed in the article. See the next image.

Once the image has been inserted into the text, the formatting can be changed by using the image icon in the editor's toolbar to add the image URL to the pop up window (if you wish to have an image URL). The Joomla! Image button will always remain the same but the image formatting in the editor might differ. This is just to show you how to insert an image to Article.

*Caution: Make sure you save all work before leaving the page. If you leave the page without saving, the changes done will not be applied to your website. Joomla! Does not resize images inserted in articles, you will need to resize your image from your computer before uploading to Joomla! or article.*

## Result

After saving you can refresh your site and will see your article on the front-end. See the next image.

## A Distinctive Article

The following items usually have to be taken into consideration when it comes to creating an article on your website:

> ➤ Text with one or more images

> ➤ Teaser text in list views with a read more link pointing to the full article page

> ➤ The article should appear on the front page and needs no menu link

> ➤ Nice to have: a scheduled publication date

> ➤ Nice to have: a printer-friendly version for visitors who would like to print the article

➢ Nice to have: an option to forward the article by email

Now that we have created the **5** Article pages for our new website using the same process as described above, we can now proceed to the next *Phase* which is **linking the created pages to Menus.**

> **Note:** *The articles we created will not be visible on the front-end until we link it to menu and published or we set them to be featured in the front-end.*

## *Phase THREE*: Linking the Created Pages to Menus

Joomla! website has different menus. The menus are in modules and these modules can be set into different position within the site. This basically reflects how you want your site to look like; you have absolute control over the look of the website. Now, **menus** can be linked to the newly created Articles (pages) and those links will be displayed on the website.

For it to appear, we need a link! → **Click** the New icon in the **Menu Manager** in the top menu (**Menu** → **Top Menu**). Click the 'Select' button next to the field Menu item type. A window with various links will pop up. Click on the **single article** link.

- You now need to select the desired article. Click the button "**Select/Change**" in the right pane to select the article. You will see a search box pop up with all articles. In case you can't find your article on the page right away, you can filter the list by typing a part of the article's title in the search box and then clicking on the title of the correct article in the result list See the next image.

- Enter a title for the link "**About Us**" and select the Top Menu in the menu location, why? Because we are still using the *Installed Sample Data* which already has all the content and modules in place. Leave the remaining options with their settings for now; we shall come back to them later.

*Caution: Make sure you save all work before leaving the page. If you leave the page without saving, the changes done will not be applied to your website.*

- Refresh your website page and when you click on the **About Us** link in the top menu you will see the **Content.** You have now successfully created your first page with a link to the menu.

Finally, when we installed the Joomla! *Sample Data* during the installation process, there is a "Home" link at the *Top Menu* by default. At this point if you refresh your site (front-end), you will notice there will be two links at the Top Menu '*HOME*' and '*ABOUT US*'. This action is to show you how to create a menu link to your site. See the next image to notice the menu changes.

All you need to do now is to repeat the '**same steps**' to create menu links to the remaining *four* articles that you created earlier. You will link each article to the new menu you create. Just follow the steps above.

> *Tip: You can write any name in the new menu. The **menu title** is what will be displayed on the top menu and not the article title. Once clicked, the article content will be shown on the website content page.*

We assume that you have now created *five* pages ready with some contents in them and the menu links connecting them by following the described steps earlier in this chapter. However, now we need:

- All other modules to be removed from the front-end (site), this will allow us to have contents related to "myfirstsite" i.e the *top menu* in which we have *five* excluding the *Home* menus in.

- When the site is visited through 'localhost/myfirstsite', the Home page will be shown. This is simply because it is set as the default homepage. We can also change the default page to be the 'About Us" page if we wish.

- All other links visible in the Menus to be removed.

See the next screenshot to understand better.

You can edit, add or delete any content of the website, to do this simply login to the administrator panel (back-end) and go to the *Article Manager* to select items to edit, delete or even add new articles and make a link to it on the front-end. It looks beautiful and yet with a simple five page website. Trust me!!!Joomla! 2.5can do even better ☺.

Finally, you should remember that you are still using the *sample data* which already have lots of menus and content created by Joomla! during installation. But now you do not want all the contents and menus on the website anymore, therefore, you have to clean up all or irrelevant menus and contents in the site.

> *Tip: For those who are familiar with Joomla!, if you want a better design, "DON NOT" install the sample data when you are installing Joomla!2.5, just make a normal installation as this will give you the chance to build your site from scratch without any predefined menus or articles. I used the sample data site to give you a better picture on how the whole Joomla! website will look like when you finish building it. You have absolute control of the site and you can design it to your requirement (subject to the kind of website you are developing).*

## *Phase FOUR: Clearing the Unwanted Menus and Articles*

To do so, **Go** to the **Menu Manager** in the **Top Menu** (*Menus → Top*). To make the process fast, click the check boxes on the left side above the menu items to choose all of them, and then click the icon *Unpublish*. After doing this, you will see all icons become *Red* on each menu item (***image1.***). At this point, if you go to your website and refresh it, you will notice that the *top menu* is no longer visible. Do the same procedure with the *Main Menu* and the *About Joomla*! menu. Choose all menu items, except the *Home* which is Front-page item.

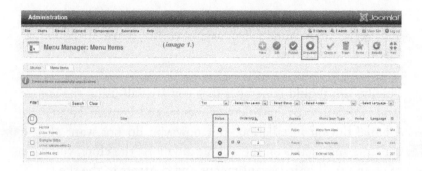

This *Home* menu item cannot be deleted because there *must* be a front-page in the site. When you also look at the lower area of the menu manager page, you may change the number of displayed menu items.

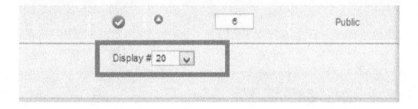

- To clear Article Use the same procedure as described above. **Go** the *Article Manager* and choose all content items to *unpublish* or delete them if you wish.

- To make sure that all data will disappear from your site, you have to clear the entire *cache* by Going to (*Site →  Maintenance → Clear Cache*). Again, choose all content and delete it.

Your Joomla! 2.5 website should now look Empty as you will notice in the next image that all *menus* are gone except the home page which is the default page and must be there.

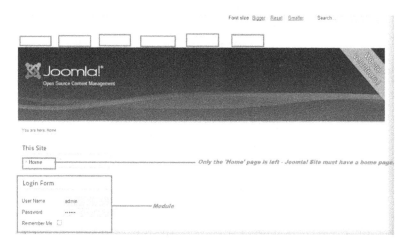

You will notice a *Login Form* on the site; this is a module and can be shifted to a different position within the website. However, we shall discuss more on modules in the coming chapters but for now if you wish to test and see how you can discard the *Login Form* module from the site. Try the following steps:

- Go to **Extensions** → **Module Manager** using the menu. The "Module Manager" lets you manage all the modules. Here you will see a list of all the currently installed modules on the site, (you get all this modules on display because you installed the *sample data* during the installation process).

- Now tick the check boxes on the left of each module name to select all of them except for "**Main Menu**", and then click on the *"unpublish"* button at the top right with the red. Doing this will hide all those modules including the *Login Form*.

At a later time, you can repeat the same process to hide all modules or menu content you wish.

*Note: "**Unpublish**" simply means that items selected will not be in use or visible within the site until set otherwise. The "**Publish**" button when clicked on a selected article, menu, module or any component means that that item will be displayed or visible on the site front-end.*

It is absolutely important that you read the steps above carefully and '**Do**' what it says when you are building your website to get the best result. Joomla! 2.5 versions are the best ever version of this popular content management system software which makes it all easy for you to design and develop your website in just minutes. The best part is that "you do not need any technical skills to develop your website using Joomla! and it's absolutely free for you", you can download Joomla! 2.5 at the official Joomla website http://www.joomla.org/download.html

Installing Joomla! is possibly the biggest problem to getting started on creating your website. However you will need to get a

WAMP server installed and of course the Joomla! 2.5 Package. Once you have these two Steps complete, it is very easy for you to use Joomla! to build and develop your website of any kind.

However, if you find this chapter to be a bit complex for you to understand because we used the *Sample Data* to demonstrate how Joomla! 2.5 works; don't worry! Subsequent chapters will simplify the whole process and then you will realize Building website with Joomla! is as easy a sipping a cup of Coffee ☺. Read on . . .

# CHAPTER 4

# Understanding Categories in Joomla! 2.5

When you create and write articles in Joomla! 2.5, you assign it to a category. Assigning articles to categories will help you not only to categorize and keep track of articles, but it also help your website visitors find similar content based upon the category of the article they're reading. This is basically the normal thing to do when writing and article.

## Can I have Sub Categories in Joomla! 2.5? (Categories of Categories)

The previous version, Joomla!1.5 used a section/category structure. This meant that every article belonged to a category, and every category belonged to a section. This was slightly limiting as it does not allow for better categorization of content. For instance, you could not have subcategories of categories. It also required that you have both a section & a category, when you basically needed just one category. Latest versions of Joomla! like the 2.5 don't use the *section & category* structure anymore. They only use categories, hence you have the capability to create sub categories of categories if need be.

Joomla! Articles must be categorized. Generally speaking, categorization is the process of recognizing, differentiating and understanding something through abs creating as many categories traction (Hagen Graf, 2012). This may sound rather complicated but proves very useful when managing several articles. Joomla! offers the possibility of creating as many categories as you wish. It is possible to build nested categories and an article has to be related to one of these categories. Newspapers, for example, use categories to better differentiate between their articles.

## To create a new category in Joomla 2.5 is very simple:

1. Login to your Joomla! Administrator panel.

2. Go to the *Content* → *Category Manager* and then click *Add New Category or simply* click the *Category Manager* in the control panel and click the New button at the top right of the page.

3. Type in the desired title for the category.

4. Choose a Parent Category.

- *Is this a Parent Category?*
  which means that If you would like this category to be a main category (one that is not a sub category of any other category), select—**No** Parent

- *Is this a Sub Category?*
  If you want this category to be a sub category of another category, then select the parent category. See below.

5. Type the Description for the category. This description will show when someone visits the category page (a page that will list all of the articles belonging to the category) this is optional though.

6. Click **Save & Close**. And that's how to create a new category in Joomla 2.5!

**Note:** *Adding a category to Joomla does not automatically add the category to any menus on your site. If you want to link this category from a Joomla 2.5 menu, you will need to create a new category menu item to the menu of your choice.*

You can select from different layouts for the articles. In the next image you can see which layout is used for which link. You can select the layout in the edit form of a menu item as shown below.

Some possible layouts:

✓ a list of all categories.

✓ a blog layout (like on the front-page).

✓ a category list.

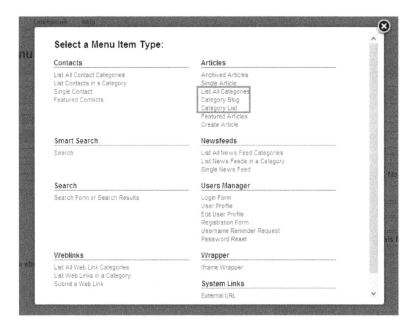

It depends on the layout you have; many options are available to configure the appearance of sub categories and articles.

# CHAPTER 5

# Creating Your Articles & Menus

One of the most important parts of a website is the content. However in Joomla! an Article is a piece of content consisting of text (HTML), possibly with links to other resources. For example, images, links etc can be within an article. Each article you have represents a category and you can have as many sub categories as you want. You can also have an *"uncategorized"* article which means it exist alone and doesn't associate with any category, yet this will be displayed on your website. These articles are maintained using the article manager in the back-end of Joomla!

## Types of Contents in Joomla!

Joomla! has contents such as *articles, categories, web links, banners, contacts and feeds.* You can also use Modules to create content. However, you may want to improve your content with files like *photos* and other media types. In this regard, Joomla! has its *Media Manager* which serves as a toolbox to manage all these contents so that it can be valuable to visitors of your website.

## Adding Content to Your Website

To create a simple page on your website, we shall be considering the *title, text, inserting an image and linking the created page* to a menu at the top of the website. To do so, **Login** to the Administrator back-end.

1. Click on the *'Add New Article'* button in the main Control Panel to open the New Article screen or, Click the *Content → Article Manager → Add New Article* in the menu item to go to the Article content area where you have to write all text you want to show.

2. Then click the **New** button to get to the applicable content editor and then add the *title* and *text*. In the upper pane, below the title, select *"uncategorized"* as a category. Note that this category was created when you install the *Joomla!*. When you see a field as *Featured* with a *Star blue like icon*, it shows that the content should be displayed in the *featured* blog layout, which is mostly used as the front page. Select **No.** In the editor window since we don't want to display the article on the front page, rather we want to link it to top menu. The default editor in Joomla! is the TinyMCE.

You will still see some articles that are *'unpublish'*, therefore they appear in red icon. After clicking '**New**' you will be taken to the new article screen which contains options for categorizing and naming the article, editing, featured (*Select NO for featured*) content and Publishing Options. In this case, just select the *uncategorized*.

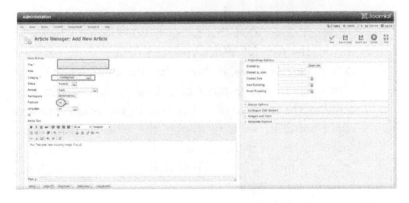

3. **Click Save & Close** when you are done typing your text in the Article Editor as seen in the image above.

## Adding Image to Article

If you want to add an *image* to your article or content, you will need to upload it from your Computer. To do this;

1. **Go** to the ***Article Manager or (Content → Article Manager)***

2. Select the article's title and the *edit Article page* will open. Below the editor window you will find the Image button. This button launches a dialog box to upload an image. You can choose between existing images or upload new ones, but first, you have to put the cursor to the point where you want the image to be placed in the article. See the next image.

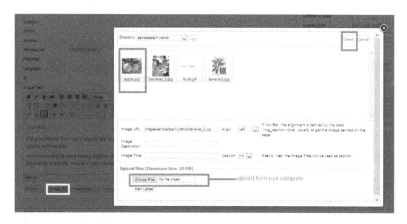

After inserting the image into the text, the formatting can be changed by using the image icon in the editor's toolbar to add the image URL to the pop up window (if you wish to have an image URL).

**Note:** *Make sure you save all work before leaving the page. If you leave the page without saving, the changes done will not be applied in your website. Joomla! Does not resize images inserted in articles, hence, you will need to resize your image from your computer before uploading to Joomla! or article.*

## The Result

After saving, refresh your site and you will see your article on the front-end. See the next image.

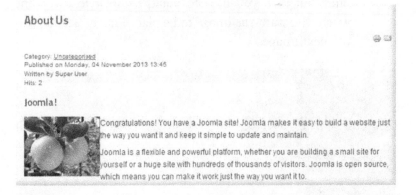

## Using the Read More in Content

Sometimes you have an article that is too large to display on the front page of your website, you probably want people to read all the articles but then only some part can be shown on the front page. This serves like intro of the article. Joomla! has a special feature called *"Read More"* which allows you to read other part of the article in full. To do this lets add a new article. You can also put an alternate text to replace the read more.

1. Follow the steps in the *"Adding Content to your website"* above. **Go** to Article Manager and select any of the articles which you want to add the *Read More* link to. Alternatively you might choose to edit an existing article to add the feature. It is allowed in Joomla!

2. Now point your cursor to any place within the article content.

3. Scroll down to the bottom of the page and click the *Read More* button.

4. Now click **Save & Close** to see the changes in the front-end. Refresh the site first.

## Linking the Article to Menu

To have a very good and usable website, you should have all your articles and content linked to menus on your website. Joomla! has a built-in system for managing menus, you will not have a good website unless there is a menu to help users navigate to different pages. You have created the article above; now do the following to link it to a menu:

1. Go to **Menus** → **Top Menu** and click **New** at the top right of the page.

2. Click the '*Select*' button next to the field Menu item type. A window with various links will pop up. Now click on the link '*Single Article*" option.

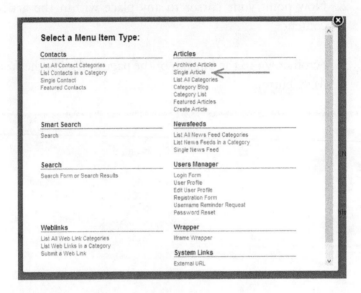

3. You now need to select the desired article. Click the button **"Select/Change"** in the right pane to select the article. You will see a search box pop up with all articles. In case you can't find your article on the page right away, you can filter the list by typing a part of the article's title in the search box and then clicking on the title of the correct article in the result list.

If you have followed this process correctly, you can now view your article on the website, however, only the *title* you set when creating the *menu* will show at the Top Menu of the site. But when a user clicks on the menu link, the Article in which you linked will be displayed.

"For example: if the article you created is titled *"I love using Joomla 2.5"* and when you created the Menu, the title is *"Joomla!"* therefore, only the menu title will be displayed on the site. So when a user clicks *"Joomla!"* on the top menu, the Article *"I love using Joomla! 2.5"* will display."

## Creating Parent Items in Joomla! 2.5

When you are building your website, sometimes you have a group of links that you only want to show after another item is clicked, Joomla! help you manage these types of groupings. We will be using the five pages we created in **Chapter Three** to describe how to create a parent Items in Joomla! *Note: We want to make Number 2 (item) the Father of 3, 4 & 5.*

1.  To do this is very simple, simply **Go** to the **"Menus"** → **"Main Menu"**

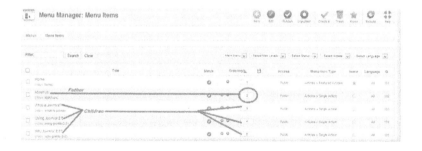

2.  Click on the item you want to be a child to another (here we click on Item 3) and you will be shown the Edit page for the Number 3 menu item.

3.  Go to the *Parent items* and select the Father (which is 2 in this case).

You have now successfully made the *"About Us"* menu the father to the *'What is Joomla!'* menu. Therefore, do the same process for Item 4 & 5.and you will notice a shift in balance to the items.

4.  Click **"Save & Close"** and you will be redirected to **"Menu item Manager"**

5.  Go to the front-end of your site and see the changes, when you click on the **Father**, it shows a list of children.

As you will see in the next image, the items have shifted under the 'About Us' Menu, therefore making it the Father to the other menus we selected.

The result of the action we just performed will be as follows.

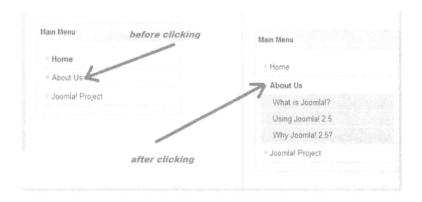

## Page Breaks—Dividing Long Article

Sometimes you have longer article and you want to divide it to make it easier to select which section of the article to read. Dividing such articles into sections is a helpful way of presenting content. Joomla! can be used to divide long Articles into multiple pages which are linked using **Previous** and **Next** page navigation and also a Table of Contents section which is displayed as part of the Article.

To divide a long Article into multiple linked pages:

1. Open the Article for editing either by:

2. Click the *Content → Article Manager* Menu item to go to the Article Manager, select the Article and click the Edit button.

3. If logged in to the Front-end, you have appropriate permissions and are viewing the Article you wish to edit: Click the Edit button.

4. Locate the position in the content where the first page should end with the cursor.

5. Click the Page break editor button at the bottom of the page.

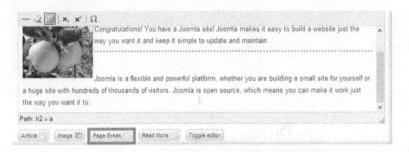

You will get an insert page break pop up page. Enter the *Page Title* and *Table of Contents* Alias as required:

1. *Page Title*: Allows you to enter a sub title for the page displayed after the Article title. If left blank the main Article title will be used.

2. *Table of Contents Alias*: Used to give a shortened name for the Table of Contents which is displayed as part of multiple page Articles. If left blank the link will be displayed as Page #.

3. Click the *Insert Page break* button. The screen will close and a horizontal rule will be inserted to show the location of the *Page break*.

4. To close the Insert Page break screen without inserting a *Page break* click the **X** close button. To remove a Page break *delete* the horizontal rule using the *delete* or *backspace* keys.

**Note:** *It is not possible to edit the Page Title and Table of Contents Alias using the content editor once it has been inserted. To modify the Page break you can do one of the following:*

- *Delete and re-insert the page break using the process described above.*

- *Edit the raw HTML of the Article using the editor and modify the title and all attributes of the relevant <hr> HTML tag.*

### Formatting Articles & Adding External link

It can be boring when visitors come to your site covered with text, Joomla! uses WYSIWYG *(what you see is what you get)* Editor that works a bit like Microsoft word. You might want to add and change some of the article looks. You can do this by selecting your article in the Article Manager or simply create a new article. You have already created an article. So simply do the following:

1. Go to *"Article Manager"* and select the article you want to format.

2. In the content area you will notice on the editor you have something like Bold (**B**) italic (*I*) underline (<u>U</u>) and so on.

3. Now let's add a link to the Joomla!

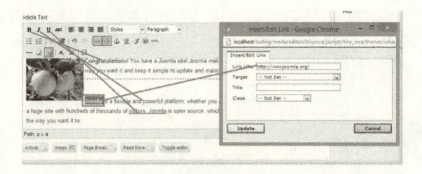

4. To insert a **link**, highlight the word you want to link to another website and click the link icon on the editor.

5. You get a pop up, type in all details including the URL address and click insert.

6. Now after editing your content. Click on *'Save'* button on the top right of the page to see changes on your site. If you are satisfied.

7. Click **Save & Close**.

## Ordering Articles

Sometimes you might want to order articles on your website. For example you have Article (1) & Article (2) on your FrontPage. Now you want A to be down and B to be on top. This is how you do it:

1. Go to the **Article Manager**

2. Use the blue arrows to push down the article or push up the article. And you are done.

3. Go to the FrontPage and view the changes. You will notice that the article you pushed down will be displayed below the other one. It depends on how you will like your orderings.

You may also use the number to set the ordering, but remember to click the icon **"Save"** at the top on the numbering.

## Deleting Articles/Contents

There are times which you want to delete some content in your website, it's pretty easy to do this in Joomla!. When you delete an article, it goes to the trash and however, that article will no longer be visible on your website. Remember, when you delete an article it goes to the *"Trash"*. To delete it permanently:

1. Go to the *'Select Status'* at the top middle of the *Article Manager* page in the back-end of your Joomla! site!

2. Select the article you wish to delete permanently and click *"Empty Trash"* it will now be deleted permanently on your website.

To restore an earlier trashed article, select the article and click on the *"Publish"* button. Joomla! will restore back your article to the article manager and your article will now be *"Published"*.

## Toolbar

The toolbar is located at the top right of the page.

The function of each tool is as follows:

- ✓ *New*. Opens the editing screen to create a new article.

- ✓ *Edit*. Opens the editing screen for the selected article. If more than one article is selected (where applicable), only the first article will be opened. The editing screen can also be opened by clicking on the Title or Name of the article.

- ✓ *Publish*. Makes the selected articles available to visitors to your website.

- ✓ *Unpublish*. Makes the selected articles unavailable to visitors to your website.

- ✓ *Featured*. Marks selected articles as featured. Works with one or multiple articles selected.

- ✓ *Archive*. Changes the status of the selected articles to indicate that they are archived. Archived articles can be moved back to the published or unpublished state by selecting "Archived" in the Select Status filter and changing the status of the articles to Published or Unpublished as preferred.

- ✓ *Check In*. Checks-in the selected articles. Works with one or multiple articles selected.

✓ ***Trash***. Changes the status of the selected articles to indicate that they are trashed. Trashed articles can still be recovered by selecting "Trashed" in the Select Status filter and changing the status of the articles to Published or Unpublished as preferred. To permanently delete trashed articles, select "Trashed" in the Select Status filter, select the articles to be permanently deleted, then click the Empty Trash toolbar icon.

✓ ***Options***. Opens the Options window where settings such as default parameters or permissions can be edited. See Article Manager Options for more information.

✓ ***Help***. Opens the help screen to guide you further.

## Batch Process

You can change one value or all three values at one time. Note that if you copy items to a new category, changes you have selected for access level and language will be applied to the copies, not the original.

To batch process a group of items:

1. Select one or more items on the list by checking the desired check boxes.

2. Set one or more of the following values:

   • To change the access levels, select the desired new access level from the Set Access Level list box.

- To change the Language, select the desired language from the Set Language list box.

- To change the Category, select a category. To leave the category unchanged, use the default value of "Select".

  ○ To copy the items to a different category, select the desired category from the category list box and check the Copy option. In this case, the original items are unchanged and the copies are assigned to the new category and, if selected, the new access level and language.

  ○ To move the items to a different category, select the desired category from the category list box and check the Move option. In this case, the original items will be moved to a new category and, if selected, be assigned the new access level and language.

3. When all of the settings are entered, click on **Process** to perform the changes. A message "Batch process completed successfully." will show.

Batch process the selected articles

If choosing to copy an article, any other actions selected will be applied to the copied article. Otherwise, all actions are applied to the selected article.

Set Access Level  - Keep original Access Levels - ▾

Set Language  - Keep original Language - ▾

Select Category for Move/Copy

Select ▾    ○ Copy  ● Move

Process  Clear

Joomla! 2.5.14

Joomla!® is free software released under the GNU General Public License.

## Setting the Article Manager Options for Articles

Joomla! provides a control panel to help set the parameter of the entire article that will be created in your website. To do this, simply:

1. Go to the **Article Manager**

2. Click on *"Option"* icon at the top right of the page, you should get a pop up page

3. You can make all necessary changes on every tab on the pop up and click **Save & Close** when you are done.

*Note: Joomla! has made basic settings for you by Default. Leave the Article Manager Options for articles as it is, alternatively make your changes in the individual article parameters.*

## Setting Individual Article Publishing Options

This section allows you to enter additional option for Article. These Options allow you to override the Article Manager Option.

A value of *'Use Global'* means that either the setting from the Menu Item or the setting from the *Global Configuration* will control the action. A setting other than *'Use Global'* will always control the action and override settings from these other areas. The setting here takes top priority. The setting in the Global Configuration controls both of the other setting that is set to *'Use Global'*. See the next image.

| ▼ Article Options | |
| --- | --- |
| Show Title | Use Global ⌄ |
| Linked Titles | Use Global ⌄ |
| Show Intro Text | Use Global ⌄ |
| Show Category | Use Global ⌄ |
| Link Category | Use Global ⌄ |
| Show Parent | Use Global ⌄ |
| Link Parent | Use Global ⌄ |
| Show Author | Use Global ⌄ |
| Link Author | Use Global ⌄ |
| Show Create Date | Use Global ⌄ |
| Show Modify Date | Use Global ⌄ |
| Show Publish Date | Use Global ⌄ |
| Show Navigation | Use Global ⌄ |
| Show Icons | Use Global ⌄ |
| Show Print Icon | Use Global ⌄ |
| Show Email Icon | Use Global ⌄ |
| Show Voting | Use Global ⌄ |
| Show Hits | Use Global ⌄ |
| Show Unauthorised Links | Use Global ⌄ |
| Positioning of the Links | Use Global ⌄ |

*Tip: If you put your cursor around the items in the article page, Joomla! has made it very easy by providing a tooltip to briefly explain what each items means. This is really helpful for beginners*

## Metadata Information

Metadata is information about the Article that is not displayed but is available to Search Engines and other systems to classify the Article. This gives you more control over how the content will be analyzed by these programs. Find below where you can put the entries.

- ○ **Metadata Description.** Optional Metadata Description for this Article.

- ○ **Metadata Keywords.** Optional entry for keywords. Must be entered separated by commas (for example, "cow, bag, and dog") and may be entered in upper or lower case. (For example, "BAGS" will match "bag" or "Bags"). Keywords can be used in several ways. You can get more details on metadata from your host provider or SEO professionals. As this is beyond the scope of this book. Other entries like the Author, content right are optional.

The Article system in Joomla! 2.5 is very powerful and very easy to use. You can easily develop your entire website by using valuable articles in a very user-friendly way. This chapter discussed how you can create articles, Menus and link both together to allow users of your website have easy navigation. The chapter also demonstrates a step by step on how to create various actions like inserting the *Read More* link in an article, *Page Breaks* and so on. At this point my assumption is you can create as many articles and menus in Joomla and link them together.

# CHAPTER 6

# Making your Site Dynamic with Component, Module & Plugins

The Joomla! 2.5 contains many built-in Extensions. By now you have already come across few of them. As a website user, you probably don't care much about the extension you are using as long as you find that it is working. Therefore, as an administrator, you have to know exactly what is going on. We have already looked at some Joomla! extensions like the *content* extension, which allows you to *write and manage articles* as well as *publish* them in different ways on your website. The user extension relates to users, the category extension to categories and so on. I am going to cover the functionality of additional extensions that are part of the Joomla core. In the Components menu, you will see Banners, Contacts, Joomla! update, Messaging, Newsfeeds, Redirects, Search, Smart Search, and Weblinks. We will have a look at '**some**' of these components including related modules and plugins.

Joomla! 2.5 comes with pre-installed components and extensions like the Banner, Contact, Joomla! update, etc. it also comes with some module like the Login module, bread crumbs, footer etc.

### What is a Component in Joomla!?

Component is one of the Extension in Joomla!. Components are the main functional units of Joomla! They can be seen as mini-applications. The components are Joomla!'s content elements or applications that are usually displayed in the center of the main content area of a template. However, this depends on the design of the template you are using. Components are core elements of Joomla!'s functionality. Some of these core elements include Joomla! Update, Contact, and Banner Component.

## Components and Extension

To really make your site look good and function well, you will have to use the Joomla! extended functionality which means that you will be using Components and Extensions menu in the back-end of your Joomla! site. However, the key difference between the two is that components are more powerful and more complex; they are actually applications within the Joomla! applications. Modules are smaller add-ons that can contain all sorts of dynamic information and sometimes components and modules are designed to work together. But the secret is that, both component and extensions generally serve the same purpose in the back-end of your Joomla! site. They enhance your website functionality!

For you to understand how to use these component in the Joomla! Website, I shall be using some that Joomla! has already. Joomla! comes with some basic components and extension that you can make use of.

## Adding the Contact Component

When you have a website and you do not properly show where you can be contacted, you are creating doubt in the minds of your users. This is very important component in every website as it enables visitors to get in touch through a contact form.

If several contact forms are needed, you should think about the underlying structure. Just like the article categories, it is possible to assign contact categories to menu items. As a result, you will see a list of contacts assigned to that category. If you click on the name or the title of these contacts, you will see more details and the form itself. As everywhere in Joomla you have the option to create nested categories and different menu item types.

In options (*Components-Contact-Options*), you can, for example, configure the appearance of the contact form (*Slider, Tab, no formatting*) and set an impressive number of other parameters. I will show you how to create a single contact, but however if you wish to create many contacts, then you have to assign them to the category in which you want them to be. Do the following:

1. Open your Joomla admin area and navigate to *Components → Contacts → Categories.*

2. Click on the **New** button and enter the details of your new contacts category. Only the Title value is required. You can also set the preferred configuration for the rest of the options.

3. **Save & Close** the changes and return to *Components →
   Contacts → Contacts.*

4. Click on the **New** icon to begin the setup of your
   Contact us page.

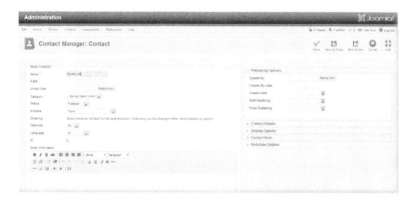

5. Enter the required values in the corresponding fields.

Review the options listed in the right part of the page and set
them based on your needs.

For you to receive a copy of the contact form inquiries, enter a
valid *e-mail* in the *Contact Options* list.

6.  **Save & Close** the Contact Us page setup and **Go** to *Menus → Main Menu* to publish it. Click on *Add New Menu* Item.

7.  Select the menu item type from the corresponding dialog

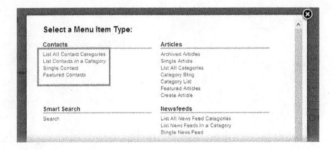

8.  Enter the *Menu Title* value and select the contact in the right part of the page by clicking on the ***Change Contact button***.

9.  Review and set the other options that are not mandatory as per your requirements.

10. **Save & Close** the new menu item and check the result on the front-end. (refresh the Page first)

## Adding Weblinks

With the weblinks component, you can create a link list or a download section that you can integrate into your website. Joomla! provides the nested categories system and counts the individual hits on the links. This component is useful for link catalogs. You may *add* as many weblink categories as you need, create as many weblinks as you have, then connect both by assigning categories. Add a menu link, choose a layout and configure the options.

The weblinks component provides three menu item type layouts: *List All Web Link Categories, List Web Links in a Category and Submit a Web Link.* We have already seen the first two layouts in articles and categories. By using the third one, you can involve your users in the creation of a joint catalog. Create a menu item *'Submit a Web Link'* in the user menu and set the permissions in *Components* → *Web Links* → *Options* to allow registered users to create links. The Options area provides six tabs full of configurable details.

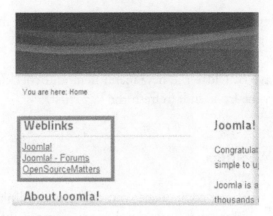

## The Banner Component

In most websites, Banners are a very popular way of advertising, especially for website that makes sales online. Joomla! has banner placement and organizational capabilities as a basic feature. This component is designed so that the webmaster can easily manipulate with banner exchange. The webmaster has information on the number of Impression and clicks i.e. will have a stored count of how many people clicks on the banner, and can also set certain banner categories as well as give authority to the clients he/she chooses.

To begin this process, you have to make configuration for the banner component in the back-end of the Joomla!. When you click on the banner, you will notice *four sub menu* that will be visible i.e. *Banner, Categories, Clients, Tracks.* Let's set up one:

1.  Before you create any clients or banner, you have to create a *Category first.* The categories are very beneficial because later on in the banner module, you can select from which client and which category a banner should be displayed.

2. To add the client **Go** to *Components* → *Banner* → *Clients* → **New** and fill in the form as required.

3. Now add the banner, Go to *Components* → *Banner* → *Banner*. And choose the *category* and the *client;* upload the banner and fill in the size. **Save & Close** when you are done.

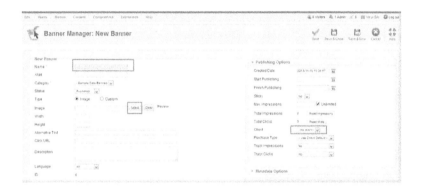

You can configure several options as you wish. Like the *Start and Finish* date for publishing the banner. This is very useful for time-limited subscription plans. There is also an option for re-setting clicks and impressions.

> **Note:** *You can set up different banners for different client in your site; this allows each client to advertise his product/service on your site. Again with this functionality, you and the client can actually track the clicks and impression statistics made on each banner on the site. It's indeed helpful.*

After creating *categories, clients and banners*, you have one more process to finish. And this is creating a module to help you display the banner in the front-end of your website. Depending on the number of Banners you want to display, you can create as many Banner modules as you wish.

To do this: **Go** to *Extensions* → *Modules* and click on **New** Icon.

1. Add the title of the banner and other configuration like position (this position depends on the template you are using) you will get more details in the *Template Chapter*.

2. Select the desired client and the Category of the banner.

3. After filling all details Click ***Save & Close*** icon on the top right of the page.

The **Search by Tag** field is an interesting feature. When it is used, the banner will be displayed when banner keywords (set in banner) and page keywords (set in article and other places) match. Another choice to control the visibility of the module and the banners is the **Menu Assignment;** you can select which menu to display the banner. One very important feature is the possibility to write a header and/or footer text. In some countries advertisements have to be labeled.

> ***Note:*** *I have selected the **position-3** on the template I am using for the sample Date (Beez2). The position depend on the template you are using and of course the position you wish to display the banner on your website*

The banner will now appear on the website (As in the next image) which is based on the configuration and number of banners you want. The banner itself is linked to the client's website, and if you move the mouse across the image, a tool tip with the banner title will be shown gives you more clue.

If you have all setting set correctly, all *impressions and clicks* of the banner will now be tracked by the banner component. This *tracking* can be viewed in *Components* → *Tracks* and you can filter it by date, client, category and type.

## Understanding Modules in Joomla! 2.5

When you install Joomla! 2.5, there are 24 built-in Modules are available for use in the front-end of your web site. Some Modules, like the Menu Module, are used in every Joomla! website. Other Modules are optional.

In this section, I will show you how to create and add some modules to your website. You will also learn how to configure the Modules.

Modules are the blocks of content in your site and are distinctively separate from your main content area. For example, a module may appear to the left, right, top, or down or below your main article content. The Module Manager allows you to customize each module to your *"Preference"*.

> **Note:** *Each module in Joomla! 2.5 has some constant features. Modules have more individual parameters but these are the most important ones to understand first.*

**Title:** The title of the module is displayed above the module on the frontend. It is also called a "Module Heading". After a Module is saved, the module's title is also shown in the Joomla! back-end administration.

**Show Title:** This setting allows you to specify whether or not the module's title should be visible on the front-end.

**Position:** A Module position may be labeled as left, right, bottom, top, etc. Module positions are defined by the template. If a Module is published in a position that is not supported by the template, it will not show up. It is important to be aware of your template's supported module positions.

**Status:** Allows you to *publish* or *unpublish* the selected module in the front-end.

**Ordering:** You can set the order of a Module to appear in the ordering dialog as well as the Module Manager main page by clicking the up/down arrows.

**Module Class Suffix:** A Module class suffix allows you to specify a preset style which is defined by the template. You'll need to consult your individual template documentation to see what module styles/suffixes are available.

*Menu Assignment:* When a Module is enabled it can be assigned to all pages or pages specified in the Menu Assignment dialog. It also means that you can limit the appearance of the module in the website.

*Start & Finish Date:* These allow you to set the stat date to display the module on the site and the end date.

*Access:* This allows you to set which group of users can use or view the module.

*Note:* You also have the option to add note to the module.

In Joomla! 2.5, all modules have (*Four*) sections; *Details, Menu Assignment, Basic Option and Advanced Options.* The **Basic Options** are different for each Module type.

## Advance Option

You may use the following:

✓ Select from different template layouts if the template offers this feature.

✓ Add a module class suffix, which adds a text to the CSS class of the module. This is useful for individual styling.

✓ Use the cache system by switching it on or off and set a time before the module is re-cached.

As I have mentioned earlier that Joomla! 2.5 has 24 built in modules, I will briefly describe them so that you can understand what each of them is for. *Note: Some of the descriptions are taken from the Joomla help resources as cited by Hagen Graf.*

***Archived Articles*:** This module offers a list of months and is linked to the archived articles.

***Articles Categories:*** This module displays list of categories from one parent category.

***Articles Category:*** This Module displays a list of articles from one or more categories.

***Articles—Newsflash*:** This module displays a fixed number of articles from a specific category or a set of categories. You may configure ordering, number of articles, read more link and many more features.

***Articles—Related Articles*:** This module displays other articles that are related to the one currently being viewed. These relations are established by the Meta Keywords.

All the keywords of the current article are compared with all the keywords of all other published articles.

***Banners*:** This module displays the active banner, which we created earlier in this chapter.

***Breadcrumbs:*** This module displays the navigation breadcrumbs, usually breadcrumbs are positioned. horizontally on the top of a web page. Two structures are used:

✓ To show links back to each previous page the user clicked through to get to the current page.

✓ To show the parent pages of the current page.

Breadcrumbs are a way to prevent visitors from being confused on your site. Basically visitors should always know where they are on the site and how to go back. Joomla! provides a breadcrumb module for such action and most of the templates have a breadcrumb position. Take a look at the Breadcrumb:

***Custom HTML*:** This module allows you to write your own HTML code and displays it in an appropriate module position.

In *Basic Options,* this module has the useful **Prepare Content** feature. Joomla! 2.5 offer the possibility to apply additional functions to article content, like email cloaking, via the plug-in mechanism. If you turn on the *Prepare Content,* the HTML content you added to the module will be treated as any article content.

*Feed display*: This module enables the display of a syndicated feed on your website.

*Footer:* This module shows the Joomla! 2.5 copyright information. You are allowed to deactivate it but you are also invited to keep it on your website. Some template providers give permission to remove their copyright information and put yours.

*Language Switcher*: This module is new in Joomla 1.6— It displays a list of available content languages for switching between them.

*Latest News:* This module shows a list of the most recently published articles. Filtering options are: by *category, author and featured articles.*

*Login Module*: This module displays a *username* and *password* login form. It also displays a link to retrieve a forgotten password. If user registration is enabled, another link will be shown to enable self-registration for users. It is possible, for example, to add additional text to the form, to redirect your user after *login* and *logout,* and to encrypt the login form using SSL, which has to be provided by the web server.

*Menu Module:* This is a container, which displays menu items of an existing menu. A menu can consist of nested menu items. You can filter these items by the start and end level, e.g., all the links from the second and third level. It is also possible to decide whether the sub menu item should be shown or not.

**Most Read Content:** This module shows a list of the currently published articles, which have the highest number of page views. You can filter by category and limit the number of articles.

**Random Image:** This module displays a random image from your chosen directory. Usually, you will use the media manager to stores these images. You can configure the file type of the image, a URL to redirect to if the image is clicked upon and you can adjust the width and the height of the images. Joomla! does not resize the original image; it only sets attributes in the *img* tag.

**Search:** This module displays a search box. You may configure the design of the box, the position and the text of the button.

**Smart Search:** This is an alternative to the Search module and displays a search box. It offers, in addition to the settings of the module Search, and the ability to define filters.

**Statistics:** This module shows information about your server installation together with statistics on the website users, number of articles in your database and the number of web links you provide.

**Syndication Feeds:** This module creates a syndicated feed for the page where the module is displayed. It displays an icon. You can enter a text to be displayed near the icon and choose the feed format (RSS 2.0, Atom 1.0).

**Weblinks:** This module displays weblinks from a category defined in the Weblinks component.

**Who's Online:** This module displays the number of anonymous users (e.g. guests) and registered users (ones logged in) that are currently accessing your website.

**Wrapper:** This module shows an *iFrame* window at a specified location. You configure the URL where the external website is located, switch scroll bars on and off, define the width and the height and give the *iFrame* a target name.

### Adding Module Custom HTML—Creating a Sidebar

This section guides you on how to create a Module to display your content in the front-end as a sidebar. You might want to add your company *"working hours"* displayed on your site. Do the following:

1. Go to **Extension** → **Module Manager** and click **New**. You will see about 24 modules available.

2. Click the **Custom HTML** Module.

3. Enter the title of the **Module (in this case; Working Hours).**

4. Select the **Module Position** (in this case; I select *position6* on template *Beez20*—Default).

5. Click on **Status** to **Publish.**

6. Leave any other settings as it is.

7. Scroll down to the bottom of the page. In the **Custom Output** Area Type the working Hours.

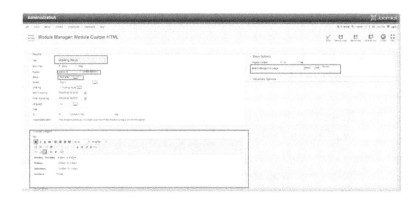

> **Note:** *You may set a background image for the Module if you wish (Basic Option)*

8. **Save & Close** and refresh the site in the front page.

You should now have a "Working Hours" Module displayed at the right side of your site. However, you may choose any position that suits you, but it depends on the template you are using.

## Adding a Login Module to your Joomla! Site

This section guides you on how to create a *Login Module* to your site which allows your visitors to register an account with you and login to the website. To do this:

1. Go to **Extension** → **Module Manager** and click **New**. You will see 24 modules available.

2. Select the **Login** module.

3. Enter the title of the **Module (Example: Please Login, Staff login Only)**

4. Select the **Module Position.**

5. Click on **Status** to **Publish.**

You may also want to configure some additional features like pre-text, post-text SSL encryption and login/logout redirection, Greetings, Menu Assignment and so on.

6. Click **"Save & Close"** if you are done setting it and **refresh** the site to see changes.

One of the benefits of the *Login Form* is that it is not necessary for the user to click a link before the log in form appears; it is displayed as a module on the side of the template. However, if you don't want to have the *Login Form* as a module, it is also possible to create it through a component. Thus you have to create *menu items* with the appropriate menu item types concerning your needs *(Menus → Main Menu → New (Users Manager))*.

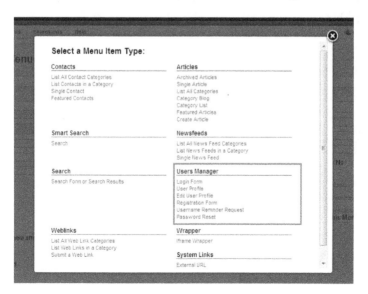

*"Basically all **Modules** are configured the same way but remember! the "**Basic Options**" for each Module Differ. So you have to set the Basic Options for each Module you want to add on your website.*

*I have briefly described all Other Modules you will see in Joomla! 2.5, however, you might want to add any of them to your website to make it more meaningful and functional for your visitors. Just follow How to Add Modules as shown in this chapter"*

## Understanding Plug-in in Joomla! 2.5

Plug-ins are used to handle login, text replacement, editors and other functions within Joomla! Site and they are very essential, but rarely noticed part of Joomla!. Plug-ins are very flexible and can execute various purposes at many different times. To locate the Plugin Manager:

**Go to Extensions-Plugin Manager,** you will see the list of the plugins available on the system. To view all the Plug-in, click on the Display at the bottom of the page and select **All.**

In Joomla! 2.5, there are various types of plug-in: *authentication, captcha, content, editors-xtd, editors, extension, finder, quick icon,*

*search, system* and *user.* These are also the names of the website sub directories where the plug-in files are located. For example, plug-ins with a type of *authentication* is located in the website directory *plugins/authentication.* It is absolutely not possible to create a plug-in in the *Administrator Panel* just like it is done in the *modules manager.* You must install plug-in through the **Extension Manager** in the back-end of Joomla! 2.5.

The plug-in covers wide varieties of functionality, you will notice on the top of the list the *Authentication Plugins,* for example if you want to enable your visitors to login to your site Using their *Username and Password.* Simply enable the **Authentication—** Joomla! (By default the Joomla! Plugin is enabled) Permission, which is always the process that follows authentication, verifies that an authenticated user has permission to do something. You authenticate with your *username* and *password,* and you are authorized by being a member of a permitted group. Joomla! offers three possibilities for authentication.

**Note:** *Be very careful with deactivating plug-ins. You must have at least one authentication plug-in enabled or you will lose all access to your site.*

> ✓ *If you don't know about a particular plug-in DO NOT make any changes to it.*

> ✓ *Do not delete any plugin that comes with Joomla! during installation.*

Just like the *Captcha* which is a new feature in Joomla! 2.5. *Captcha* is a program that can tell whether its user is a human or a computer. You might have come across them yourself; they are colorful images with distorted text at the bottom of Web registration forms. They are used by many websites to prevent abuse from "bots, Bots according to Wikipedia is a software application that runs automated tasks over the Internet or automated programs usually written to generate spam. No computer program can read distorted text as well as humans can, so bots cannot navigate sites protected by captchas. The plug-in uses Google reCAPTCHA service to prevent spammers. To get a public and private key for your domain, visit http://google.com/recaptcha.

To add a captcha to new account registration, go to *Options* in the *User Manager* and select *Captcha* → *reCaptcha*.

- If you want to edit some of the plugins, simply click on the plug-in and edit it and then click *save& close.*

- If you want to make the plugin function in your site, make sure you set it as enabled or else you won't be able to see any changes in your site. Remember not all plug-ins have a physical effect on your website but they are very important for your site.

To read more about Plugin go to:

✓ http://forum.joomla.org—Sign up for the forums, search, and ask questions, even helping others if you are able!

✓ http://help.joomla.org—Find more documentation and training information.

**CHAPTER 7**

# Using Templates & Extensions for Your Joomla! Site

Template is one of the most significant Joomla! extensions that changes the looks and feel of your website and is one of the determining factor that makes a visitor of your site continue to navigate and explore the website. If your website design is great, visitors definitely will expect the rest to be great as well. However, your template design for your website will depend on target groups, for instance: A newspaper website is expected to have a website that have much text to allow users to read in details what is going on around the world. Again if your company is involved in Travel & Tourism, definitely your target group does not want to see text but Pictures that are attractive.

There are two types of templates in Joomla!: *Front-end Templates* and *Back-end Templates*. However changing the style of your Joomla! Website is very easy through templates. When you install a template; the menu, modules and contents are still same but the colours and styles will be different.

*"There are many site devoted to free Joomla! Template and you surely can download as many as you want; all you have to do is go to a search engine like Google and type in Free Joomla! 2.5 Template and many free templates will appear."*

When you finally get a Template that you like, download it to your computer, it will come in a "Zip File" when you have the zip file, now go and login to the *Administrator Panel* in the back-end of your Joomla!2.5 site. You are now set to install the Downloaded *Template*.

## Installing Joomla! 2.5 Template

1. Login to the back-end of your site "localhost/
   yoursitename/administrator/" or (*www.your-site.com/
   administrator/*) when you are using the live host. (live
   host means you have purchased a domain name and host
   account from a company for your website)

2. Click on: **Extensions Manager → Install**

You can install all your *Templates, Plugins, Modules,
Components and Languages*. You have three options:

- ✓ *Upload Package File*—(select a package from your PC,
  upload & install it).

- ✓ *Install from Directory*—(enter the path where the
  package is located on your server).

- ✓ *Install from URL*—(enter the URL to the package).

> **Note:** *We will use the first method which is the Upload Package
> File to install the Template as it is most suitable.*

3. **Select** the package from your PC and click the button "**Upload File & Install**"

If the package contains no errors you are done and you will get a "*Success Message*". *In case of error contact the template provider or ask questions in Joomla! Forum.*

**To locate your newly installed template you do the following:**

1. Go to *Extension Manager* → *Template Manager. You will see the entire installed template including the Default Templates that come with Joomla! After installation.*

2. Select the newly installed Template.

3. Click the *Yellow Star* at the top right of the Template Manager. The template is now set as the default for the site *Front-end*.

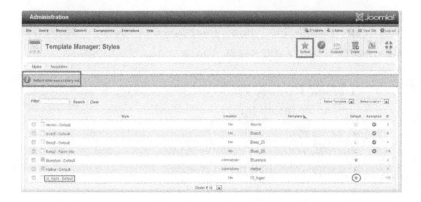

## The Result in the Front-end

All the contents are the same from above view of the new template. When a template is changed, only the look and feel of the site changes, but not the contents.

*"There are times when you install and change the template of your site, some **Modules** and **Components** disappear. This is because every template has its design and module positions. The*

*best way to organize your site is to see the various module positions of the template; this will help you in organizing your website."*

To view the template *Module Positions* from the back-end of your Joomla! 2.5 site, you must first enable *Preview Module Position* from the **Template Manager Options**

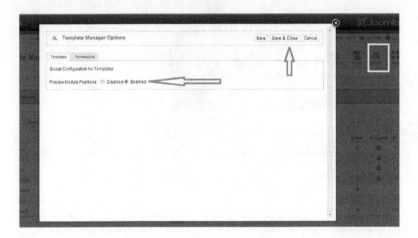

After that action, you will be *redirected* to the *Template Manage: Style*

- Now put your cursor just by the icon close to the template in which you want to view the module positions. See below:

- Select and click on the Default Template (That is; the template u are using for your site)

*I am using the new template installed for this illustration.*

- Click on **Preview** of the Template as seen in the previous Image.

**Note**: *Description of some of the toolbar for the Template Manager is as follows:*

The Descriptions are: (*These contents are from the Joomla! Help*)

1. **Make Default**. Makes the selected template style the default.

2. **Edit**. Opens the editing screen for the selected contact. If more than one contact is selected (where applicable), only the first contact will be opened. The editing screen can also be opened by clicking on the Title or Name of the contact.

3. **Duplicate**. Makes a copy of the selected template style. The copy is created immediately and is given the same name as the original but prefixed with "Copy of" and/or suffixed with a number (eg. "(2)") so that it can be distinguished from the original and any other copies.

4. **Delete**. Deletes the selected template styles. Works with one or multiple template styles selected.

5. **Options**. Opens the Options window where settings such as default parameters or permissions can be edited.

6. **Help**. Opens this help screen.

Joomla! is known for its easiness. A single page is generated in Joomla! by the HTML output of one component, several modules and the template. Every page is accessible through a unique URL. When you look at the site front-end for instance, the content component produces the HTML output for the articles in the middle. The blocks you see in the next image are modules and they can be positioned anywhere in the template, but of course depends on you. Have a look at the module Blocks:

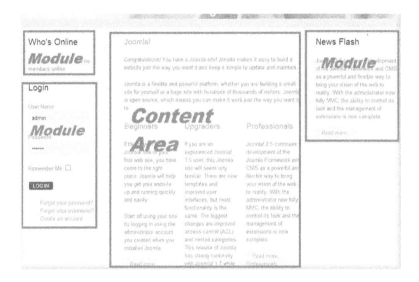

It is important that you check the *preview* of any template you are using for your website because it will assist you to arrange your modules properly and give it a great presentation. Remember having a well-designed and arranged website is a great way of attracting your visitors to keep exploring your website. For more information on how to utilize template in Joomla 2.5, please go to http://forum.joomla.org/ you will definitely get answer to your question (if any) from the great Joomla! community.

## Extensions

Joomla! 2.5 can be easily extended and customized just like previous versions. For those who are not familiar with extensions in Joomla! I will highlight some importance of *components, modules, plug-ins, templates and languages* through which you can extend the functionality of your site. When I said Extend, I meant adding some cool features and functions to your website to enhance user experience when they navigate to your website.

***Joomla! Components:*** This provides the most extensive functionality of all extensions. Components can totally change the functionality and look of a Joomla! website. For instance, with a component you can turn part of your Joomla! site into an online store (*E-commerce),* forum or photo gallery.

***Joomla! Modules:*** If you want just minor functionality extension such as adding a block in your pages for showing the Time, Statistics. Each module can be published in predefined blocks or template positions which differ for each template.

***Joomla! Plug-ins:*** Are invisible to the end user since they don't show directly in parts of your site. However, plug-in are very powerful and can change Joomla! input & output in various ways. An example of a plugin is the one used in user registration, *ReCaptcha* which is used in Joomla! to authenticate the user is real.

***Joomla! Templates:*** They are used for changing the look of your site. There are templates for the *front-end & back-end.* However, most templates are for the front-end since the backend template is accessed only for users with special permissions (example: *Supper Administrators).* By default, Joomla! 2.5 comes with *3 front-end and 2 back-end templates.* You can get thousands of Joomla! 2.5 templates for free online but some are commercial versions.

***Joomla! Languages:*** You will need an additional language pack in case you plan to create your site in a language different from English, which is the default one.

When looking for Joomla! extensions it is important to make sure that the one you choose is compatible with your Joomla! version. Joomla! 2.5 does not support extensions for previous versions, unlike Joomla! 1.5 that supports legacy mode and can be compatible with lesser version like the Joomla! 1.0.

*Note: All instruction and step-by-step guide in this book is for Joomla! 2.5 versions only*

## Managing Joomla! 2.5 Extensions

You can enable, disable and uninstall extensions. You can enable or disable extensions, but all the related data are still kept. If you uninstall an extension, it will be deleted. Joomla! 2.5 extensions are managed form the administrator panel.

The above image shows each tab in the ***Extension Manager*** and basically each have its function, you can understand some tabs easily but however, I will briefly explain some of the tabs here;

**Install:** This tab offers you 3 ways to install a new extension—upload a file, use a file already uploaded to your site or directly download an extension from a URL.

**Update:** This is new feature which will allow you to update Joomla! and its extensions directly from the admin panel.

> **Note:** *It is strongly recommended that you be very careful using the "Update" since the feature is new and you should always create backups beforehand. It may severely damage your Joomla! site and wipe out all its files.*

**Manage:** You can use this tab to enable, disable and most significantly uninstall extensions. It is important to know that this is the only place in the Administrator Panel that allows you to uninstall an extension. You might be confused if you are used of previous Joomla! Versions like 1.5

**Discover:** It's a new function which can detect incomplete Joomla! extensions installations. Warnings:—This screen will show you errors related to your extensions and their installation. These errors could be anything from missing files to incompatibility with other extensions or the core Joomla! installation.

**Warnings:** Error messages related to installations and updates will appear in this area. If you can't solve the problem by yourself, Post on Joomla! Forum or ask Uncle Google ☺ . . . . You'll usually find a solution or guidance on how to overcome the problem.

# CHAPTER 8

# Working with Users & Permissions in Joomla! 2.5

T his chapter will guide you through the *User Management of your Joomla! 2.5 site* to deal with different situation that will arise in your role as content editor and web master.

A website without users in considered a useless site. First you will need someone who will be responsible for managing the website and also other users who could be your customers or just random visitors who usually are directed to your site via search engines or social media websites. To manage registered users of your website can be a difficult process, especially if you have a large number of users, all of whom have different roles to perform. Each role or user profile has access to certain information or tasks within the scope of your website. You have the tools to determine the extent of their access by using the back-end interface modules. When someone registers on your website, the user becomes an automatic member of *Permission Group*. However these groups have predefined permissions and belong to an *access level*. One *Access Level* can have any number of *Permission Groups*. One group can have any number of *users/visitors. You can pass down permissions and can be overwritten in different places within the Joomla! Website.*

## Administrators—(Back-end Users)

These are users that can edit and update the website content by login into the *administration control panel* of the website. The *Manager, Administrator or Super Administrator* has different access. For example, the *Super Administrator* have absolute control over the website while the *Manager* does not have absolute access to the website, he has limited access. However, there are various levels of access and permission within the *administration control panel*, the highest level is the **Super Administrator** and only he/she can add another *Super Administrator*.

**Managers**: *They are NOT allowed to do the following:-*

   ✓ Install modules and components.

   ✓ Upgrade a user to super administrator or modify a super administrator.

   ✓ Work on the menu item Site-Global Configuration.

   ✓ Administer users.

   ✓ Send a mass mailing to all users.

   ✓ Change and/or install templates and language files.

**Administrators:** They are NOT allowed to do the following:-

   ✓ Work on the menu item Site | Global Configuration.

   ✓ Send a mass mailing to all users.

   ✓ Change and/or install templates and language files.

   ✓ Upgrade a user to super administrator or modify a Super administrator.

## Front-end Users (Website Users)

These users do not have access to the ***Administration Panel*** i.e. the back-end; they can only access material and information through the actual front-end. These users can be:

1. *Registered users, authors, editors, and publishers who have been given the privileges to edit and update information only from the front-end.*

2. *Guests or casual visitors to your site. These visitors come to your site anonymously and unregistered.*

3. *People who register their details in order to subscribe, buy or transact with you.*

When a user is registered with you, they are allocated to a group; this is based on the settings applied within the *Global Configuration*. This gives permission to visitors to register on your website to become registered member of the site. They can be any one of the following:

***Registered Group:*** A registered user can login, edit his credentials and see parts of the site that non-registered users cannot see.

***Author Group:*** The author can do everything that a registered user can. An author can also write articles and modify his or her own content. There is generally a link in the user menu for this.

***Editor Group:*** The editor can do everything that an author can. An editor can also write and edit all articles that appear in the front end.

***Publisher Group:*** The publisher can do everything that an editor can. A publisher can also write articles and edit every piece of information that appears in the front-end. Additionally, a publisher can decide if articles to be published or not.

> **Note:** *None of the above mentioned user groups have access to the Administrator Panel of the website.*

When you are using Joomla! 2.5 to build your website, it is absolutely up to you to configure your user groups. However, in the ***User Manager*** → ***User Groups*** you should have the view of all groups available.

The above setting is good enough for your website, but you may change the setting if you don't like it as it is. It is also same setting as the Joomla! 1.5. *User Groups* can be given access levels. Hence, a user connected to a group is connected to an access level.

## User Registration

When you install your Joomla! 2.5, you had your first registration process. Remember in the final step you were prompted for a *username, email address* and a *password?* The person who installed Joomla! is considered *Super Administrator,* who has permission to do whatever he/she want on the site. You as the supper administrator can now modify the behavior of the site in *Users-User Manager* → *Options* as seen in the next image.

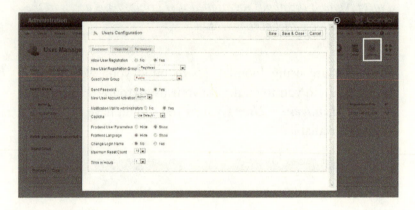

## Registered Users Only Access

Many people want the ability to only allow registered users to access certain pages in their site. Joomla! 2.5 makes it very easy to block access from the public and only allow registered users the ability to access certain pages. To do this:

1. **Go** to your Joomla! 2.5 *Admin Panel,* open for edit either the article or menu item that you want to prohibit access on.

2. Next to *Access,* in the drop down change *Public* to *Registered.*

3. Click *Save & Close* in the top right menu.

After this action is done, whenever visitor tries to view the page that is no longer set for *public*, they will be asked to Login.

## Disabling User Registration in Joomla! 2.5

If your website doesn't have anything like e-commerce, or community site, then it's not important to have the option to allow people to register in your site. Therefore to disallow people from registering, do the following:

1. **Go** to your Joomla! 2.5 A*dmin Panel.*

2. Click the *User Manager* icon.

3. Click the *Options* icon in the top right of the page.

4. In the *Component tab*, set *Allow User Registration* to **No** and then click "**Save & Close**"

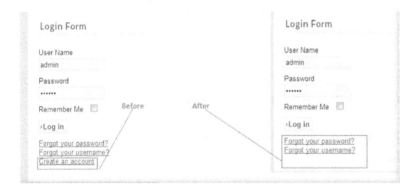

You have now disabled user registration! Your Joomla 2.5 website will no longer have the new user registration option. You will observe that the "*Create an account*" link is missing, you only have "*forgot your password?*" and "*forgot your username?*"

link. This is because you have set the allow user registration to be "**No**" in the Global configuration of the user setting.

### Creating New Joomla! 2.5 Administrator

During the installation of Joomla!, the one user that was created is the *Supper Administrator*, however, sometimes it might be difficult for you alone to manage the website so you want to add another Administrator to help in managing the Joomla! site. To do this:

1.  **Go** to your Joomla! 2.5 *Admin Panel*.

2.  Click *User Manager*, then click ***Add New User*** and enter the required information under (*username, email and password*).

3.  Under *Assigned User Groups*, select **Super Users** (by default it will be Under Registered—Uncheck that option).

4.  Click **Save & Close** when you finish.

### Changing User's email Address in Joomla! 2.5

If you intend to change your email address in Joomla! Do the following

1.  **Go** to your Joomla! 2.5 *Admin Panel*.

2.  Click *User Manager*, and then click.

3.  Search the user to be edited, click on the *username*.

4. Update the **Email** address, and then click **Save & Close.** Repeat the same if you have other users to edit their details.

## Adding User Notes

This is a new feature in Joomla! 2.5 which allows you to creates notes with review dates for each user. One good thing about this feature is that it allows you to setup a workflow process; also other Administrators can see these notes.

To add the user note:

1. **Go** to your Joomla! 2.5 *Admin Panel.*

2. Click *User Manager*, and then click.

3. Click the *User Notes* tab, and then click **New** in the top right menu.

4. Under *New Note*, fill in the required fields, and then click **Save & Close** in the top right menu.

## Mass Mail

This feature is used to send emails from the Back-end of your Joomla! website. It allows you to select and send emails to users from different *User groups*. To use the mass mail user component, you have to configure Joomla! for sending emails in Global *Configuration → Server → Mail settings*. You may then configure the Subject Prefix and the Mail body Suffix in *Users → Mass Mail Users: Options → Mass Mail*. It's really easy to understand the mass mail user component; you can also choose the group you want to send mail to from the available user groups. Simply key in message and send to *User Group* concerned.

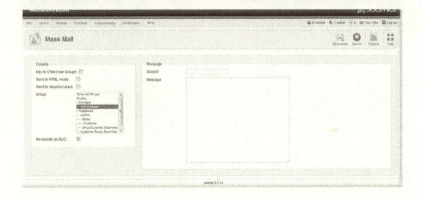

After you have filled up necessary information on the form, click "***Send Email***". And your email will be sent to the group you chose.

**CHAPTER 9**

# Understanding Global Configuration, Check In & Statuses

*G*lobal *Configuration* is the area of the Joomla! administrative interface where a user with Super Administrator features is able to make changes that globally affect the behaviour of the web site and also alter some default settings for the presentation of, and access to site content.

All the parameters under the *Site, System* and *Server* tabs in the Global Configuration are stored as values in the file *configuration.php*, which you will find in the root folder of Joomla! installation. This file is set up automatically by the software installation process and thus many of the parameters appearing in the Global Configuration screens are best left as their initial settings.

The work area of the global configuration is divided into **(5)** tabs and every tab consists of various fields and check boxes, text areas and switches. Joomla! Makes things easy for you because you could move your cursor around each item or field and you can get a tooltip (a short description) that could really help you through.

As I have mentioned earlier, the settings in the global configuration is best left untouched, however if you must perform some changes, make sure you have knowledge of it. I will describe some of the setting in the *global configuration* for you to understand better.

**Site Setting:** This tab allows you to change all basic site settings such as *site name, Meta data and SEO options*. You can also put your *site offline* and set the *offline message* from here. You may also decide to upload an image as your offline message so it doesn't need to show the Joomla! Image. All options are important in the Site tab, especially the SEO ones.

**System Setting:** Most of the settings in the system tab are slightly advanced; you should definitely pay attention to two of them:

✓ *Cache Settings*: Set it to On-Progressive Caching if you'd like maximum caching and fastest Joomla!. Set it to On-Conservative if you'd like to disable modules caching. In any case there is cache time in minutes. During this time changes may not appear because cached copies will be served to the viewers.

✓ *Session Settings*: This is the timeframe during which you will stay logged in your Joomla! even if you are inactive. Increase it if you are annoyed by being logged out too often from your Joomla.

**Server Settings:** These settings are the same like that of Joomla! 1.5. This parameter has three options: *"None"*, *"Administrator Only"*, and *"Entire Site"*. Using the appropriate setting, this parameter forces any web browser connections to the administrative *"back-end"*, or to the complete Joomla! site, to use the secure HTTP protocol (HTTPS). The *"Entire Site"* setting is appropriate where security of any web transaction (example: e-commerce) is important. Preferably there should also be suitable certificate in place to verify the identity of your website. The *"Administrator Only"* setting is ideal for enhancing the security of other types of website as it encrypts *"back-end"* content and *passwords* that could be put to malicious use if intercepted.

> **Note:** *If you decide not to use the default setting which is 'None', then it is important that you check the server delivering your website is capable of operating in HTTPS mode.*

**Permissions:** This setting is very crucial to your website as it gives you the chance to basically allow, deny and inherit the permissions—*Site Login, Admin Login, Offline Access, Super Admin, Access Component, Create, Delete, Edit, Edit State and Edit Own.* Every group has their own set of permissions. By default you should NOT change anything in the Permissions for a standard site. These functions are rather meant for sites with complex structure and multiple user levels.

**Text Filters:** Websites can be attacked by users entering in special HTML code. Filtering is a way to protect your Joomla! website. Filtering options give you more control over the HTML that your content providers are allowed to submit. You can be as strict or as liberal as you desire, depending on your site's needs. It is important to understand that filtering occurs at the time an article is saved, *after* it has been written or edited. Depending on your editor and filter settings, it is possible for a user to add HTML to an article during the edit session only to have that HTML removed from the article when it is saved. This can sometimes cause confusion or frustration. If you have filtering set up on your site, make sure your users understand what types of HTML are allowed. The default setting in Joomla! 2.5 is that all users will have "*black list*" filtering on by default. This is designed to protect against markup commonly associated with website attacks. So, if you do not set any filtering options, all users will have "black list" filtering done using the default list of filtered items. If you create a filter here, this overrides the default, and the default filter is no longer in effect.

## Check In

This is a new feature in Joomla! 2.5. Even those who are familiar with the Joomla! 1.5 will find it tricky when using Joomla! 2.5. However, this great feature is a security feature for editing your content. Once you start editing content, Joomla! locks the content for all other users. For instance, you are the *Super Administrator* and you are editing an Article page, another User who is a manager cannot open that Article because it only allows you to act on it, the manager can only have access to the Article after the *Super Administrator* have saved and close the article. The good thing about this action is that changes by another user cannot be overwritten. A big problem may arise if a user is editing the content and unintentionally closes the browser window, allows the session to expire or maybe laptop battery is drained and shut down the laptop. Then the content will be locked and no one else can edit it! No one else unless you have proper permission, for example; you as the *Super Administrator or Administrator* can check in the content again to allow others to edit it. When content is locked, you will only notice the content by a small lock being displayed near the title. I personally find this feature to be cool . . . ☺

Have a look at two *locked* module in the next image:

## Statuses

Contents in Joomla! 2.5 can have several statuses. This basically depend on the type of content, there can be as small as three statuses: *Published, Unpublished & Trash.* Bear in mind that after you create and save a new content, it exists in the Joomla!

database and based on its status, it will appear 'or not' in different areas of your Joomla! website.

Occasionally it is necessary to *trash* contents or *unpublish* them. The content itself will continue to exist even if it is trashed, because trashing doesn't mean it has been deleted. You can filter most of the tables in the administration interface by the desired statuses and assign different statuses to your content as much as you like. *A brief description of the items in the Content Statuses*;

**Published:** It depends on the *'users and visitors'* permissions whether they will be able to view the content, but generally the content on your website should be visible because it has been published!

**Unpublished:** No website visitor is able to see the content. It is the phase in which you edit and review your content.

**Featured:** The featured *'feature'* is a switch you can use for your most important and latest content and is usually shown in the front-page of your website. It is an additional status because it is only relevant to *articles*.

**Archived**: Occasionally you might want *archive* for your articles. Just set the status to archived and you've almost created an archive. Joomla! knows the creation date of your articles and offers an archive module to be shown on your site. The archive module is included in the example data. If you have a new site without the Archived module, you can create from **Modules →** **New → Archived Article.** Follow the steps in module creation as discussed in earlier chapters to get it done.

# CHAPTER 10

# Exporting & Importing Joomla! 2.5 Database from your PC to another PC

B y now you should know that Joomla! 2.5 consist of TWO components. The Joomla! files and the Database. These files and folders of your Joomla! applications contains the scripts and core applications codes, while the Joomla! Database contains all records of your website such as articles, Media, Videos, Categories, and Images.

To perform this task, I assume you have a WAMP webserver installed.

- So click on your server Icon at the bottom right of your taskbar and click on the "*phpMyAdmin*", you should see a screen that looks like this:

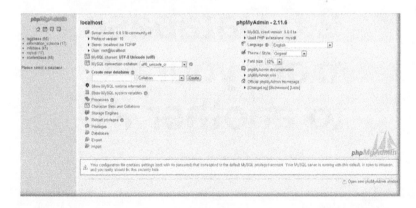

**Note:** *This process is for the localhost Database transfer from one PC to another PC. Do this if you want to continue building your website in another Computer. However, if you want to transfer your database from your personal computer to another host company, you will have to contact them for further assistance.*

You should see a list of the databases available on the top left column. Click on the link to your Joomla! database, i.e. the database that you wish to export. In this example, the database is "mfsbase". Once you have clicked on your Joomla! database, you will be shown a screen like this:

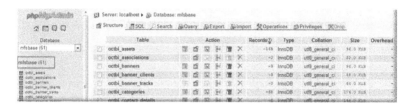

Make sure the database you choose is the right one for the Joomla! files and folders, i.e. your website. Do **NOT** delete any of the tables. Click on the tab labelled *"Export"*, and you will be shown a screen like this:

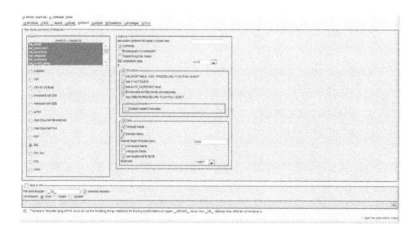

## Exporting Process

The trick happens here. Follow these simple steps, and you will have your database exported to an SQL file and saved on your PC (computer).

1. *Select all of your Joomla! tables from the list of tables. It is selected by default, so leave it as it is.*

2. *In the list of export types, make sure "SQL" is selected. It is selected by default. (This makes it easier to re-import your data later.)*

3. *Leave your SQL options as they are.*

4. *Make sure "**Save as file**" is checked at the bottom of the page.*

5. *Click the button labelled "**Go**" in the bottom right of the page.*

6. *Save your ".sql" file to your system and make note of where you saved it. I recommend saving it on your desktop for easy access. You might decide to change the location later for security reason.*

You are done with the export. You should now have a file on your system that is an exact copy of your Joomla! database.

## Importing the Saved Copy into a New Database

You'll first need to create the new, empty database on your server (i.e. the new computer). Use the same database name you have exported to your PC, we used "mfsbase". After the new database has been created:

1.  *Go to phpMyAdmin page via your WAMP server (localhost).*

2.  *Click the database name on the top left-hand side of the page.*

3.  *Select the Import tab.*

4.  *Click the Browse button under "File to import", then select the database file from your computer.*

5.  *Click **Go** (bottom of the page) to import the database.*

*__Caution:__ If you see a "No database selected" error, it's probably because you forgot to first click on the database name in the left-hand column.*

After successfully transferring your Database to your new computer, Also you have to copy the Website folder from the location **C:wamp** → **www** in your old PC and paste in same location in the new PC.

You can now **GO** to your browser and type for Example: 'localhost/myfirstsite' or 'localhost/yoursitename' and you will be directed to your website.

It is important that you note that same process applies to you hosting your Joomla! Website to a live server—in this case, your **Host Company** will guide you with necessary steps to upload your newly developed Joomla! 2.5 website.

This chapter teaches you how to **Export** your Joomla! database in your personal computer, have it saved (*for backup*) and **Import** it to another Computer. This can only be executed if you have localhost in your computer, if you encounter any problem transferring Joomla! 2.5, ask in the Joomla! Forum and am sure your problem will be solved. http://forum.joomla.org/

# Credits

*Joomla! : http://www.joomla.org/*

*Hagen Graf : www.cocoate.com*

*Immotion Hosting : http://www.inmotionhosting.com*

*Siteground : http://www.siteground.com/*

*Learn Joomla : http://www.learnjoomla.co.uk*

# Appendix A:
# Key Resources

**Book**—Building Website With Joomla! 1.5 in 60 minutes—http://www.traffordpublishing.com.sg/books/BUILDING-WEBSITE-WITH-Joomla.aspx

Joomla—http://www.joomla.org/

WAMP (Windows)—For more information, visit http://en.kioskea.net/download/download-1318-wamp-server

Download Joomla! 2.5. x—http://www.joomla.org/download.html

Joomla! Extensions Directory: Find an extension—http://extensions.joomla.org/

Joomla! Forums: Get support.—http://forum.joomla.org/

Technical Requirements: Get ready to install—http://www.joomla.org/technical-requirements.html

Joomla! Core Features—http://help.joomla.org/ghop/feb2008/task020/Joomla!%20Core%20Features%20V1.2.pdf

Learn Joomla—http://www.learnjoomla.co.uk/blog/brand-new-learn-joomla-25-book-launched

Joomla24 Templates—http://www.joomla24.com/

Free Templates—http://www.joomlashack.com/products/free-joomla-templates

## JOOMLA HOSTING COMPANIES

Siteground Web Hosting company—http://www.siteground.com/

GreenGeeks—http://www.greengeeks.com/

justhost.com—http://www.justhost.com/

FatCow—http://www.fatcow.com/fatcow/special-promo.bml?LinkName=No_Name

Hostgator—http://www.hostgator.com/

# Appendix B:
## Some Organizations that Uses Joomla!

UNISEL University Selangor—
http://www.unisel.edu.my/

Guaranty Trust Bank Uses
Joomla—http://gtbank.com/

Malaysia Immigration—http://
www.imi.gov.my

Monaco yacht show—http://www.
monacoyachtshow.com

Barnes & noble—
https://nookdeveloper.
barnesandnoble.com

U.K ministry of defense—http://
www.stabilisationunit.gov.uk

High Court Of Australia Uses
Joomla www.hcourt.gov.au

Eiffel Tower Uses Joomla—http://
www.tour-eiffel.fr/

*And many more at http://
joomlagov.info/*

# About the Author

 Abdulkadir Shehu is a practicing Joomla! trainer in Kuala Lumpur, Malaysia.

He holds a BSc. (Hons) in Business Information System at University of East London and Master of Business Administration (MBA) from Anglia Ruskin University—UK. Having worked in the web design and education industry for many years, he has been educating colleagues, friends and clients about the effectiveness of using Joomla! in website development.

Mr. Shehu has been conducting Joomla! training for companies, business owners, students, and individuals to name just a few, to help them build and maintain their Joomla! websites.

When not working, he takes pleasure in making new friends and loves sharing his knowledge with others. He is a Nigerian and currently lives in Kuala Lumpur, Malaysia with his family. This is his second book.